BRIGHT NOTES

AS YOU LIKE IT BY WILLIAM SHAKESPEARE

Intelligent Education

Nashville, Tennessee

BRIGHT NOTES: As You Like It
www.BrightNotes.com

No part of this publication may be used or reproduced in any manner whatsoever without written permission, except in the case of brief quotations in critical articles and reviews. For permissions, contact Influence Publishers http://www.influencepublishers.com

ISBN: 9781-6-45425-52-6 (Paperback)
ISBN: 9781-6-45425-53-3 (eBook)

Published in accordance with the U.S. Copyright Office Orphan Works and Mass Digitization report of the register of copyrights, June 2015.

Originally published by Monarch Press.
Rainer Pineas, 1964
2020 Edition published by Influence Publishers.

Interior design by Lapiz Digital Services. Cover Design by Thinkpen Designs.

Printed in the United States of America.

Library of Congress Cataloging-in-Publication Data forthcoming.
Names: Intelligent Education
Title: BRIGHT NOTES: As You Like It
Subject: STU004000 STUDY AIDS / Book Notes

CONTENTS

1)	Introduction to William Shakespeare	1
2)	Introduction to As You Like It	12
3)	Textual Analysis	16
	Act 1	16
	Act 2	31
	Act 3	49
	Act 4	62
	Act 5	75
4)	Character Analyses	101
5)	Critical Commentary	113
6)	Essay Questions and Answers	122
7)	Bibliography	129

INTRODUCTION TO WILLIAM SHAKESPEARE

FACTS VERSUS SPECULATION

Anyone who wishes to know where documented truth ends and where speculation begins in Shakespearean scholarship and criticism first needs to know the facts of Shakespeare's life. A medley of life records suggest, by their lack of inwardness, how little is known of Shakespeare's ideology, his beliefs and opinions.

William Shakespeare was baptized on April 26, 1564, as "Gulielmus filius Johannes Shakspere"; the evidence is the parish register of Holy Trinity Church, Stratford, England.

HUSBAND AND FATHER

On November 28, 1582, the Bishop of Worcester issued a license to William Shakespeare and "Anne Hathaway of Stratford" to solemnize a marriage upon one asking of the banns providing that there were no legal impediments. Three askings of the banns were (and are) usual in the Church of England.

On May 26, 1583, the records of the parish church in Stratford note the baptism of Susanna, daughter to William Shakespeare. The inference is clear, then, that Anne Hathaway Shakespeare was with child at the time of her wedding.

On February 2, 1585, the records of the parish church in Stratford note the baptisms of "Hamnet & Judeth, sonne and daughter to William Shakspere."

SHAKESPEARE INSULTED

On September 20, 1592, Robert Greene's A Groats-worth of witte, bought with a million of Repentance was entered in the Stationers' Register. In this work Shakespeare was publicly insulted as "an upstart Crow, beautified with our ["gentlemen" playwrights usually identified as Marlowe, Nashe, and Lodge] feathers, that with Tygers hart wrapt in a Players hyde [a **parody** of a Shakespearean line in II *Henry VI*] supposes he is as well able to bombast out a **blank verse** as the best of you: and being an absolute Johannes factotum, is in his own conceit the only Shake-scene in a country." This statement asperses not only Shakespeare's art but intimates his base, i.e., non-gentle, birth. A "John factotum" is a servant or a man of all work.

On April 18, 1593, Shakespeare's long erotic poem *Venus and Adonis* was entered for publication. It was printed under the author's name and was dedicated to the nineteen-year-old Henry Wriothesley, Earl of Southampton.

On May 9, 1594, another long erotic poem, *The Rape of Lucrece*, was entered for publication. It also was printed under Shakespeare's name and was dedicated to the Earl of Southampton.

On December 26 and 27, 1594, payment was made to Shakespeare and others for performances at court by the Lord Chamberlain's servants.

For August 11, 1596, the parish register of Holy Trinity Church records the burial of "Hamnet filius William Shakspere."

FROM "VILLEIN" TO "GENTLEMAN"

On October 20, 1596, John Shakespeare, the poet's father, was made a "gentleman" by being granted the privilege of bearing a coat of arms. Thus, William Shakespeare on this day also became a "gentleman." Shakespeare's mother, Mary Arden Shakespeare, was "gentle" by birth. The poet was a product of a cross-class marriage. Both the father and the son were technically "villeins" or "villains" until this day.

On May 24, 1597, William Shakespeare purchased New Place, a large house in the center of Stratford.

CITED AS "BEST"

In 1598 Francis Meres's Palladis Tamia listed Shakespeare more frequently than any other English author. Shakespeare was cited as one of eight by whom "the English tongue is mightily enriched, and gorgeouslie invested in rare ornaments and resplendent abiliments"; as one of six who had raised monumentum aere perennius [a monument more lasting than brass]; as one of five who excelled in lyric poetry; as one of thirteen "best for Tragedie," and as one of seventeen who were "best for Comedy."

On September 20, 1598, Shakespeare is said on the authority of Ben Jonson (in his collection of plays, 1616) to have been an actor in Jonson's *Every Man in His Humour.*

On September 8, 1601, the parish register of Holy Trinity in Stratford records the burial of "Mr. Johannes Shakespeare," the poet's father.

BECOMES A "KING'S MAN"

In 1603 Shakespeare was named among others, the Lord Chamberlain's players, as licensed by James I (Queen Elizabeth having died) to become the King's Men.

In 1603 a garbled and pirated *Hamlet* (now known as *Q1*) was printed with Shakespeare's name on the title page.

In March 1604, King James gave Shakespeare, as one of the Grooms of the Chamber (by virtue of being one of the King's Men), four yards of red cloth for a livery, this being in connection with a royal progress through the City of London.

In 1604 (probably) there appeared a second version of *Hamlet* (now known as *Q2*), enlarged and corrected, with Shakespeare's name on the title page.

On June 5, 1607, the parish register at Stratford records the marriage of "M. John Hall gentleman & Susanna Shaxspere," the poet's elder daughter. John Hall was a doctor of medicine.

BECOMES A GRANDFATHER

On February 21, 1608, the parish register at Holy Trinity, Stratford, records the baptism of Elizabeth Hall, Shakespeare's first grandchild.

On September 9, 1608, the parish register at Holy Trinity, Stratford, records the burial of Mary Shakespeare, the poet's mother.

On May 20, 1609, "Shakespeares Sonnets. Never before Imprinted" was entered for publication.

On February 10, 1616, the marriage of Judith, Shakespeare's younger daughter, is recorded in the parish register of Holy Trinity, Stratford.

On March 25, 1616, Shakespeare made his will. It is extant.

On April 23, 1616, Shakespeare died. The monument in the Stratford church is authority for the date.

BURIED IN STRATFORD CHURCH

On April 25, 1616, Shakespeare was buried in Holy Trinity Church, Stratford. Evidence of this date is found in the church register. A stone laid over his grave bears the inscription:

Good Frend for Jesus Sake Forbeare, To Digg The Dust Encloased Heare! Blest Be Ye Man Yt Spares Thes Stones, And Curst Be He Yt Moves My Bones.

DEMAND FOR MORE INFORMATION

These are the life records of Shakespeare. Biographers, intent on book length or even short accounts of the life of the poet, of necessity flesh out these (and other) not very revealing notices from 1564-1616, Shakespeare's life span with ancillary matter such as the status of Elizabethan actors, details of the Elizabethan theaters, and life under Elizabeth I and James I. Information about Shakespeare's artistic life-for example, his alteration of his sources-is much more abundant than truthful insights into his personal life, including his beliefs. There is, of course, great demand for colorful stories about Shakespeare, and there is intense pressure on biographers to depict the poet as a paragon of wisdom.

ANECDOTES-TRUE OR UNTRUE?

Biographers of Shakespeare may include stories about Shakespeare that have been circulating since at least the seventeenth century; no one knows whether or not these stories are true. One declares that Shakespeare was an apprentice to a butcher, that he ran away from his master, and was received by actors in London. Another story holds that Shakespeare was, in his youth, a schoolmaster somewhere in the country. Another story has Shakespeare fleeing from his native town to escape the clutches of Sir Thomas Lucy who had often had him whipped and sometimes imprisoned for poaching deer. Yet another story represents the youthful Shakespeare as holding horses and taking care of them while their owners attended the theater. And there are other stories.

Scholarly and certainly lay expectations oblige Shakespearean biographers often to resort to speculation. This may be very well if biographers use such words as conjecture, presumably, seems, and almost certainly. I quote an example of this kind of hedged thought and language from Hazelton Spencer's *The Art and Life of William Shakespeare* (1940); "Of politics Shakespeare seems to have steered clear ... but at least by implication Shakespeare reportedly endorses the strong-monarchy policy of the Tudors and Stuarts." Or one may say, as I do in my book *Blood Will Tell in Shakespeare's Plays* (1984): "Shakespeare particularly faults his numerous villeins for lacking the classical virtue of courage (they are cowards) and for deficiencies in reasoning ability (they are 'fools'), and in speech (they commit malapropisms), for lack of charity, for ambition, for unsightly faces and poor physiques, for their smell, and for their harboring lice." This remark is not necessarily biographical or reflective of Shakespeare's personal beliefs; it refers to Shakespeare's art in that it makes general assertions about the base - those who lacked coats of arms-as they appear in the poet's thirty-seven plays. The remark's truth or lack of truth may be tested by examination of Shakespeare's writings.

WHO WROTE SHAKESPEARE'S PLAYS?

The less reputable biographers of Shakespeare, including some of weighty names, state assumptions as if they were facts concerning the poet's beliefs. Perhaps the most egregious are those who cannot conceive that the Shakespearean plays were written by a person not a graduate of Oxford or Cambridge and destitute of the insights permitted by foreign travel and by life at court. Those of this persuasion insist that the seventeenth Earl of Oxford, Edward de Vere (whose descendant Charles Vere recently spoke up for the Earl's authorship of the Shakespearean plays), or Sir Francis Bacon, or someone else wrote the Shakespearean plays. It is also argued that the stigma of publication would besmirch the honor of an Elizabethan gentleman who published under his own name (unless he could pretend to correct a pirated printing of his writings).

BEN JONSON KNEW HIM WELL

Suffice it here to say that the thought of anyone writing the plays and giving them to the world in the name of Shakespeare would have astonished Ben Jonson, a friend of the poet, who literally praised Shakespeare to the skies for his comedies and tragedies in the fine poem "To the Memory of My Beloved Master the Author, Mr. William Shakespeare, and What He Hath Left Us" (printed in the First Folio, 1623). Much more commonplace and therefore much more obtrusive upon the minds of Shakespeare students are those many scholars who are capable of writing, for example, that Shakespeare put more of himself into *Hamlet* than any of his other characters or that the poet had no rigid system of religion or morality. Even George Lyman Kittredge, the greatest American Shakespearean, wrote, "Hamlet's advice to the players has always been understood - and rightly - to embody Shakespeare's own views on the art of acting."

In point of fact, we know nothing of Shakespeare's beliefs or opinions except such obvious inferences as that he must have thought New Place, Stratford, worth buying because he bought it. Even Homer, a very self-effacing poet, differs in this matter from Shakespeare. Twice in the *Iliad* he speaks in his own voice (distinguished from the dialogue of his characters) about certain evil deeds of Achilles. Shakespeare left no letters, no diary, and no prefaces (not counting conventionally obsequious dedications); no Elizabethan Boswell tagged Shakespeare around London and the provinces to record his conversation and thus to reveal his mind. In his plays Shakespeare employed no rainsonneur, or authorial mouthpiece, as some other dramatists have done: contrary to many scholarly assertions, it cannot be proved that Prospero, in *The Tempest* in the speech ending "I'll drown my book" (Act V), and *Ulysses,* in *Troilus and Cressida* in the long speech on "degree" (Act II), speak Shakespeare's own sentiments. All characters in all Shakespearean plays speak for themselves. Whether they speak also for Shakespeare cannot be proved because documents outside the plays cannot be produced.

As for the sonnets, they have long been the happy hunting ground of biographical crackpots who lack outside documents, who do not recognize that Shakespeare may have been using a persona, and who seem not to know that in Shakespeare's time good **sonnets** were supposed to read like confessions.

Some critics even go to the length of professing to hear Shakespeare speaking in the speech of a character and uttering his private beliefs. An example may be found in A. L. Rowse's *What Shakespeare Read and Thought* (1981): "Nor is it so difficult to know what Shakespeare thought or felt. A writer, Logan Pearsall Smith, had the perception to see that a personal tone of voice enters when Shakespeare is telling you what he thinks, sometimes almost a raised voice; it is more obvious again when he urges the same point over and over."

BUT THERE'S NO PROOF!

Rowse, deeply enamoured of his ability to hear Shakespeare's own thoughts in the speeches of characters speaking in character, published a volume entitled Shakespeare's *Self-Portrait, Passages from His Work* (1984). One critic might hear Shakespeare voicing his own thoughts in a speech in *Hamlet;* another might hear the author in *Macbeth*. Shakespearean writings can become a vast whispering gallery where Shakespeare himself is heard hic et ubique (here and everywhere), without an atom of documentary proof.

"BETTER SO"

Closer to truth is Matthew Arnold's poem on Shakespeare:

> Others abide our question. Thou art free. We ask and ask - thou smilest and art still, Out-topping knowledge. For the loftiest hill, Who to the stars uncrowns his majesty, Planting his steadfast footsteps in the sea, Making the heaven of heavens his dwelling Spares but the cloudy border of his base To the foiled searching of mortality; And thou, who didst the stars and sunbeams know, Self-schooled, self-scanned, self-honored, self-secure, Didst tread the earth unguessed at. - Better so....

Here Arnold has Dichtung und Wahrheit - both poetry and truth - with at least two abatements: he exaggerates Shakespeare's wisdom - the poet, after all, is not God; and Arnold fails to acknowledge that Shakespeare's genius was variously recognized in his own time. Jonson, for example, recorded that the "players [actors of the poet's time] have often mentioned it as an honor to Shakespeare, that in his writing (whatsoever he penned) he never blotted a line" (*Timber*), and of course there is praise of Shakespeare, some of it quoted above, in Meres's *Palladis Tamia* (1598).

THE BEST APPROACH

Hippocrates' first apothegm states, "Art is long, but life is short." Even Solomon complained of too many books. One must be, certainly in our time, very selective. Shakespeare's ipsissima verba (his very words) should of course be studied, and some of them memorized. Then, if one has time, the golden insights of criticism from the eighteenth century to the present should be perused. (The problem is to find them all in one book!) And the vast repetitiousness, the jejune stating of the obvious, and the rampant subjectivity of much Shakespearean criticism should be shunned.

Then, if time serves, the primary sources of Shakespeare's era should be studied because the plays were not impervious to colorings imparted by the historical matrix. Finally, if the exigencies of life permit, biographers of Shakespeare who distinguish between fact and guesswork, such as Marchette Chute (*Shakespeare of London*), should be consulted. The happiest situation, pointed to by Jesus in Milton's *Paradise Regained*, is to bring judgment informed by knowledge to whatever one reads.

AS YOU LIKE IT

INTRODUCTION

BACKGROUND AND SOURCE OF AS YOU LIKE IT

As You Like It was first published in a collected edition of Shakespeare's works known as the First Folio. (Generally speaking, a folio is a very large book.) The play was written between June 1599 and August 1600. Shakespeare took the plot of *As You Like It* from a pastoral romance by Thomas Lodge called Rosalynde, first published in 1590. (A pastoral romance is a long prose tale of love and adventure in which shepherds woo shepherdesses in witty and sophisticated language.) Shakespeare followed the plot of Rosalynde fairly closely, but while Lodge's story was a serious pastoral romance, Shakespeare's play is a **satire**; it makes fun of pastoral life. Shakespeare also added characters, such as William, Audrey, Jaques, and Touchstone. The addition of the last two completely changes the tone of Lodge's original story.

PLOT OUTLINE OF AS YOU LIKE IT

Orlando, youngest son of a deceased gentleman, has been deprived of his inheritance by his eldest brother Oliver. When

Orlando demands the money from his brother, the latter decides to have him killed in a wrestling match to take place on the next day. Orlando and Oliver live in the country of Duke Frederick, who has just usurped the throne from his brother, Duke Senior. Duke Senior and his friends have been banished, and they are living in the nearby Forest of Arden. Duke Senior's daughter Rosalind has remained behind at Frederick's court because of her friendship with Frederick's daughter Celia.

By telling a lot of lies about him, Oliver incites Charles, a professional wrestler, against his younger brother. However, to everyone's surprise, when the match takes place on the next day, Orlando is the victor. The match has been watched by Duke Frederick and his court, as well as by Rosalind and Celia. When Frederick learns that Orlando is the son of a former enemy of his, he coldly dismisses him. But Rosalind has fallen in love with Orlando, and she gives him a chain from her neck to wear as a keepsake. In turn, Orlando too has fallen in love with Rosalind at first sight.

As Rosalind and Celia are sitting in a room in the palace, Duke Frederick bursts in and orders Rosalind to leave his court at once. He is afraid that people will rally to her side and demand that her father be brought back to the throne. Because of her affection for her cousin, Celia decides to accompany her into exile. For the sake of safety, Rosalind disguises herself as a man and calls herself Ganymede. Celia disguises herself as a servant girl and calls herself Aliena. The girls decide to take Touchstone, a court jester, with them, and they set out to find Rosalind's father in the Forest of Arden.

Meanwhile, Orlando returns to his brother's house, where he is warned by Adam, an old family servant, that Oliver has planned to murder him that night. To save his life, Orlando leaves his home and sets out into the unknown, accompanied by Adam.

Rosalind and her companions arrive in Arden, where they meet two shepherds, Corin and Silvius. Corin is old; Silvius is a young man very much in love with a shepherdess called Phebe. Orlando and Adam also arrive in the Forest of Arden. Adam is almost dying of hunger, so Orlando sets out to seek some food. He comes upon Duke Senior and his companions, who take care of him and Adam.

When Duke Frederick finds that Celia and Touchstone have left his court with Rosalind and is told that all three may be in the company of Orlando, he sends for Oliver and tells him to find his brother and bring all of the fugitives back.

In the forest Orlando has been expressing his love for Rosalind by hanging love poems to her on the trees. She finds the poems and then overhears Orlando in conversation with Jaques, a companion of Duke Senior who is constantly criticizing everyone and everything. Through the conversation she learns that Orlando is the author of the poems and is in love with her. In her disguise as Ganymede, she engages Orlando in conversation and offers to cure him of his love for Rosalind. He is to come to her every day and pretend that she is Rosalind. When he woos her she will treat him so badly that she will make him furious and thus cure him of his love. Touchstone, meanwhile, has met a country wench called Audrey, whom he wishes to marry for purely sexual reasons.

While waiting for Orlando to appear for his first lesson, Rosalind and Celia are taken by Corin to watch Silvius wooing Phebe. Phebe rejects all of Silvius' advances with great scorn, which makes Rosalind very angry. When she reprimands Phebe for her cruelty to Silvius, Phebe falls in love with Rosalind, who is still disguised as the young man Ganymede. Orlando finally arrives and, after being scolded by Rosalind for being late, is given his first lesson. When he leaves, Silvius comes in with a letter to Rosalind from Phebe. Phebe has pretended to Silvius that she hates Rosalind and that the letter he is carrying is a challenge to a duel, but when he hears the letter read aloud, the unhappy shepherd realizes that it is a love letter.

Orlando is again late for his second lesson. After some time, a stranger approaches Rosalind and says that he comes with a message from Orlando. The stranger turns out to be Oliver, who was sent by Frederick to find Orlando and the others. Oliver says that he was lying sleeping under a tree in the forest and was just about to be attacked by a snake and a lion, when Orlando came along and saved his life. Because of this, the two brothers have been reconciled. Oliver and Celia fall in love with each other at first sight. Rosalind tells Orlando that she is a magician and can see to it that his Rosalind will be transported to the forest the next day, so that he can marry her when Oliver marries Celia. Rosalind also tells Phebe that if by tomorrow she still wants to marry her she may, but that if for any reason she does not want to marry her, she must marry Silvius. Phebe agrees. Touchstone and Audrey also arrange to be married along with the rest.

On the next day Rosalind reveals her true identity to her father and to Orlando. Orlando will be married to her, Oliver to Celia, Touchstone to Audrey, and, when she sees Rosalind is really a woman, Phebe agrees to marry Silvius. Just as the ceremonies are about to begin, word is brought that Duke Frederick, who had come to Arden with the intention of killing his brother, has been converted by a hermit and has decided to become a hermit too, returning to his brother the throne stolen from him. Jaques decides to remain with Frederick in Arden. The rest return joyfully to the court.

AS YOU LIKE IT

TEXTUAL ANALYSIS

ACT 1

ACT 1: SCENE 1

The scene takes place in the garden of Oliver, eldest son of a deceased gentleman, Sir Rowland de Boys. Oliver's youngest brother, Orlando, is complaining to Adam, the old family retainer, that Oliver has cheated him of his inheritance. Sir Rowland had left Orlando a thousand crowns and charged Oliver to see to it that Orlando would receive a good education. But while Oliver had sent a second brother, Jaques, to school, he had neither given Orlando the thousand crowns which were due him nor done anything at all about his education.

Orlando declares that he will no longer tolerate his brother's injustice. Just then Oliver himself enters, and the two brothers quarrel about the terms of their father's will. Words soon lead to blows, until finally Orlando seizes Oliver by the throat and forces him to listen to his demands. Orlando demands that he receive either an education befitting a gentleman or the money left to him by his father. Grudgingly, Oliver agrees to give Orlando the money, and with a "Get you with him, you old dog," to Adam, orders his youngest brother out of his sight.

> Comment

The opening of the play establishes the basic conflict between Oliver and his brother Orlando, which eventually motivates Orlando to flee to the Forest of Arden, where the main action of the play takes place. We already tend to like Orlando and dislike Oliver, if for no other reason than Orlando's friendship with the obviously "good" character Adam, contrasted with Oliver's harsh treatment of the old servant.

Left alone on stage, Oliver reveals in a short aside that he intends to get even with Orlando and that he has no intention of giving him any money.

> Comment

The aside is a short version of the soliloquy. During a soliloquy a character thinks aloud on stage. Two important **conventions** of the soliloquy are:

1. Any other characters on stage (if there are any) do not hear what is said in a soliloquy or aside.

2. In a soliloquy a character always tells the truth as he knows it; no matter how much he may be trying to deceive fellow characters, he will not try to deceive himself (or his audience).

Oliver then calls in Charles, a professional wrestler, who has come to discuss a wrestling match to be held the next day. We learn from Oliver in another aside that he has decided to get rid of his troublesome brother by having Charles kill him in the forthcoming match. However, instead of coming directly to the point, Oliver first asks Charles what news there is at Court. We learn that the rightful Duke of the land (called Duke Senior in the play) has been banished by his younger brother Frederick and has fled with some of his loyal followers to the Forest of Arden. However, he has left his daughter Rosalind behind at the usurper's Court because of her affection for her cousin Celia, daughter of Duke Frederick. According to Charles, the banished Duke and his men are having a very pleasant time in the forest, where they are completely free from all cares, as if they were living in the Garden of Eden.

Comment

The conversation between Oliver and Charles provides us with some necessary background information for the plot and reveals further the character of both Oliver and Orlando. The relationship between the two Dukes, who are brothers, should be compared to that between Orlando and Oliver. In both cases, one brother deprives the other of what is rightfully his: in the one instance, a Dukedom; in the other, an inheritance. Here is also established the relationship between Rosalind and Celia, which is to bring both of them to the Forest of Arden.

Charles has come to try to get Oliver to dissuade Orlando from entering the wrestling contest, for fear he will get hurt. Oliver replies that he has already tried to do this very thing, but that Orlando will not listen to him. Oliver goes on to tell

Charles that Orlando is a thoroughly evil character, envious and revengeful, who will stop at nothing to hurt someone by whom he imagines he has been injured. In fact, says Oliver, "and almost with tears I speak it," he has even plotted against me, his own brother, so that if you can kill him tomorrow in the match, I shall breathe more easily. Charles is very obliged for the information and promises that Orlando will get what he deserves.

After Charles leaves, Oliver admits in a soliloquy that his brother is really kind and generous, and that it is for these very qualities that he hates him so much. For even Oliver's own servants love Orlando more than they do their master.

Comment

Oliver reveals himself to be a typical Shakespearean villain by admitting his brother's goodness, but at the same time seeking to injure him. Thus he admits, in effect, that he is evil. In this admission of his intended victim's virtue and of his own evil, he is comparable to *Macbeth*, who admits that Duncan is a noble king, and then proceeds to murder him; to Iago, who praises Othello's virtues even while plotting his ruin; and to Edmund in *King Lear*, who praises his brother Edgar to the audience, while busily trying to have that same brother disinherited. There are basically two reasons for this seemingly strange behavior of Shakespeare's villains:

1. Shakespeare's plays do not attempt to be realistic in the sense that many modern plays do. When Shakespeare wants to give the audience some information, he will usually employ any source available, even if it means that someone will be speaking out of character. Thus, when

the information which has to be imparted concerns a certain character's evil nature, even so unlikely a source (from a modern point of view) as that character himself will inform the audience.

2. Shakespeare was writing in an environment in which there was little, if any, doubt about what was evil and what was good. Unlike today, there was only one accepted standard, and the person who deviated from that standard could have no doubt that he had done so. While Shakespeare was not even attempting to write realistic plays, these confessions by villains probably were not regarded as quite so unrealistic by an Elizabethan audience as they are by today's audience. Confessions of guilt before execution, when there was no earthly advantage to be gained by such a confession, were very common in sixteenth-century England.

ACT 1: SCENE 2

We find Celia and Rosalind on the lawn in front of Frederick's palace. Celia is trying to cheer up Rosalind, who is sad at the banishment of her father. Celia says that Rosalind's sadness shows that she likes Celia less than Celia likes her, for had their positions been reversed, Celia would still have been happy so long as she and her cousin were not parted. In fact, says Celia, when her father dies, she will restore everything to Rosalind that was taken from the banished Duke. Rosalind agrees to try to be cheerful and suggests that falling in love might relieve her sadness. Celia replies that falling in love is a good idea so long as it is done only for fun and does not become serious.

Comment

Shakespeare, having previously reported the affection existing between the two girls, now shows us how close their friendship is. We get some indication of Celia's warm and generous nature. Rosalind's suggestion about love's healing power foreshadows one of the principal **themes** of the play, which is concerned with various types of love, the most important of which is the love between Rosalind and Orlando. Celia's warning against falling seriously in love is ironic, for both girls (one almost immediately, the other later on in the play) fall deeply in love and forget their resolves.

At this point they are joined by Touchstone, the fool or jester of the play. Then comes a fop, Monsieur le Beau, whom Touchstone and the girls make fun of.

Comment

Touchstone is one of the most important characters of the play; his very name reveals his function. Just as a touchstone is used to test the purity of gold and silver, so does the unshakable common sense of Touchstone test the stability of the other characters. Some are mad for love, some with hate; some are all affectation, some are just stupid. His sanity is the criterion by which they are all judged.

Le Beau represents the Elizabethan gallant or affected man-about-town. The over-elaborate manners, dress, and speech of his type were often satirized in Tudor and Stuart literature. Other characters of this type are the anonymous lord in I *Henry IV* who annoys Hotspur after the Battle of Holmedon, and Osric in *Hamlet*.

Le Beau tells them that if they remain where they are, they will be able to see a wrestling match. This match, which Duke Frederick and his Court have come to watch, is the one between Orlando and Charles. Charles has already defeated three challengers and left them almost dead. Frederick has tried to dissuade Orlando from competing "In pity of the challenger's (Orlando's) youth," but without success. Now he asks Rosalind and Celia to make one last attempt, because he has no doubt that Orlando's fate will be that of the three previous challengers. The moment Celia sees Orlando she thinks he is too young to oppose Charles, and yet he has an air of success about him. The girls call Orlando to them, and Celia urges him to withdraw his challenge, as there can be little doubt of the outcome. Rosalind hits on an idea to preserve the young man's reputation; she will petition the Duke to stop the series of wrestling matches completely. In this way, no one will know that Orlando has withdrawn. But Orlando insists on going ahead with the bout. He gallantly excuses himself to the girls, hoping they will not take it unkindly that he would deny anything to two such beautiful ladies, and asks them for their support. He explains that no matter what happens to him, he could not be worse off than he already is: if he is defeated he will not lose honor or reputation, for he never had any; if he is killed, he will only have lost life, which he has never loved; and he can do his friends no wrong, for he has none. The girls are touched: Rosalind exclaims, "The little strength that I have, I would it were with you," to which Celia adds, "And mine, to eke out hers."

The match begins. Celia and Rosalind enthusiastically support Orlando. After some scuffling, there is a great shout from the audience: the mighty Charles lies prone on the ground. To everyone's surprise, Orlando has won. The Duke is about to praise Orlando for his fine performance, but when he hears that Orlando's father was Sir Roland de Boys, a friend of the banished Duke, he coldly dismisses him. Celia is ashamed of her father's behavior. Rosalind declares that had she known whose son Orlando was, she would have implored him with tears not to risk his life against Charles. Celia decides to make up for her father's unkindness by approaching Orlando and encouraging him. She tells him he has done well and adds that if he keeps his promises in love the way he has exceeded all promises in the match, his lady would be a happy woman.

Comment

There is no doubt that, up until the end of the play, the impression we are to get of Duke Frederick is that of an out-and-out villain. His sympathetic concern over the fate of Orlando before the wrestling match is therefore somewhat surprising. It seems likely that Shakespeare is here less interested in consistent character portrayal than in emphasizing the danger Orlando is facing and in arranging his introduction to the two girls. This is brought about by the Duke's request to the girls to warn the young man once more.

Rosalind, more and more taken with the young man, gives him a chain from her neck as a keepsake, declaring that she, like Orlando, is "out of suits with Fortune," and would like to give him more, but has nothing else to give. She stops short and asks Celia to leave with her. In an aside Orlando reveals he is very much impressed with Rosalind - so much so that he finds himself speechless and unable to thank her. After a few steps Rosalind pretends to Celia she has heard Orlando calling them back. In an aside she, in her turn, reveals how affected she is by Orlando: "My pride fell with my fortunes,/ I'll ask him what he would." (She refers to her lack of pride because she, the girl, is taking the initiative with the man.) She returns to tell

Orlando that he has wrestled well and overthrown more than his enemies (meaning, of course, her heart). In another aside Orlando reveals that he, like Rosalind, has fallen in love at first sight (a typical occurrence in Shakespearean romantic comedy).

Comment

The falling in love of Orlando and Rosalind is the basis for most of the action which takes place in the Forest of Arden. In Rosalind's rejection of the conventional idea that the man must take the initiative in courtship, we already see traits of her character and her attitude towards the code of courtly love, which is even more prominently displayed later in the play.

Le Beau approaches Orlando to warn him that he should leave the place immediately: because of Orlando's parentage, Duke Frederick might plan to do him harm. Orlando takes the occasion to ask the courtier which of the two girls is Frederick's daughter. He learns about Celia and Rosalind and their affection for each other, which caused Rosalind to remain behind at the usurper's Court. He is told further that Frederick has begun to dislike Rosalind because she is very popular with the common people, who pity her for her father's sake, and that the Duke's anger against Rosalind is likely to come to a boil very soon.

Comment

Le Beau's warning about Frederick's changing attitude toward Rosalind prepares the audience for the events of the next scene, in which Rosalind is banished. It also serves further to prejudice us against the Duke.

Orlando ponders his plight: "Thus must I from the smoke into the smother [thick smoke]/ From tyrant Duke unto a tyrant brother." However, he comforts himself with the thought: "But heavenly Rosalind!"

Comment

Orlando's final **couplet** in the scene shows that Shakespeare intended the audience to compare the two villains of the play. Shakespeare's scenes very often end in rhymed couplets. He did this for a very practical reason. If the actor delivered his final line in mid-stage and then, turning his back on the audience, walked toward the exit in complete silence, the effect would be ludicrous. Thus, he usually moved toward the exit while delivering his last lines. This meant that he moved farther and farther away from the audience as he talked; consequently, his very last line, delivered right at the exit, was difficult to catch. However, the audience, having heard the line before the last and knowing that the two would **rhyme**, had a good chance of piecing it out. And, the **rhymes** also serve as exit cues to alert the players of the next scene.

ACT 1: SCENE 3

Celia and Rosalind are sitting in a room in Duke Frederick's palace. Rosalind has evidently been sitting in silence for quite some time, for Celia wonders why her cousin is so quiet. Not realizing what has happened between Orlando and Rosalind, Celia thinks Rosalind is still sad about her father's banishment. Rosalind, however, tells her that it is on her own account she is sad: "Oh, how full of briers is this working-day world!" When Celia advises Rosalind to shake herself to make the burrs fall off,

Rosalind responds that the burrs are in her heart. "Hem them away" (cough them up), advises Celia. "I would try if I could cry hem and have him," replies Rosalind. Celia now gets the point and wonders how Rosalind could have fallen in love so suddenly.

Comment

Much of the humor in the play derives from witty conversation between the main characters, and much of that witty conversation consists of various kinds of word play, such as puns. The Elizabethans were highly delighted with humor derived from the manipulation of language, because they were coming to be very proud of their native tongue. They had not always been proud of it. At the beginning of the sixteenth century, if a writer had anything serious to say, the chances were rather good he would say it in Latin instead of English, for people were not at all sure that so barbarous and rude a language as English would survive for any length of time. And who wanted to write in a language which succeeding generations would be unable to read? However, with the growth of nationalism (which will be discussed later), the various nations of Europe began to rival each other in their vernacular tongues. Englishmen felt, for instance, that since Dante had glorified the Italian language by writing *The Divine Comedy*, it was up to Englishmen to uphold the honor of their country by making their language beautiful and producing great works of literature written in it. By the time Shakespeare started to write, much had been done in this direction; it had been demonstrated that English could be as literary a language as Latin, Greek, French, or Italian. So Shakespeare was writing just at the time when the English language had come of age, when people were tremendously proud of their native language, and when writers liked to play with words as children do with new toys.

The conversation between Rosalind and Celia is interrupted by Duke Frederick, who bursts into the room and abruptly orders Rosalind to leave his Court within ten days or suffer death. When the startled Rosalind asks what offense she has committed, the Duke tells her that, as the daughter of the banished Duke, he regards her as a possible rallying point for a rebellion against him. When Celia protests, her father tells her that she is a fool - she should hate Rosalind, for the people pity her and are thus more attached to her than to Celia herself: "She robs thee of thy name." But so strong is Celia's affection for her cousin that she warns her father if he banishes Rosalind he must banish her too, for she "cannot live out of her company." Frederick does not believe Celia will carry out her threat and remains firm in his resolve: Rosalind is to be banished.

Comment

Duke Frederick dislikes Rosalind for basically the same reason Oliver dislikes Orlando - she is too popular, and he feels her popularity detracts from his own. Also, as a usurper, he feels (in common with more famous Shakespearean usurpers, such as Claudius [Hamlet's uncle] and *Macbeth)* unsure of his position; usurpation teaches others the way to power. Apart from any personal shortcomings he might display, the fact that Frederick is a usurper would immediately brand him as evil in the eyes of the Elizabethan audience. It was the Stuarts who were so foolish as to proclaim the theory of the Divine Right of Kings (kings are appointed by God, not by the people; therefore, they cannot be removed by the people), and for their pains lost the throne; it was the Tudors who practiced that theory without bothering to proclaim it, and consequently retained their power.

Every God-fearing Englishman in the sixteenth century knew that it was the duty of the king to rule and of the subject to obey. The subject was responsible to the king, and the king was responsible to God. If the subject committed a crime, it was up to the king to punish him. If the king committed a crime, it was only God who could punish him, and it was certainly none of the subject's business to do anything about it. In fact, the subject who rebelled against the king or sought to oust him and take his place for any reason whatever, no matter how wicked the king, was guilty not only of treason, but also of sacrilege against God; for he was rebelling against God's appointed representative. The fact that *As You Like It* is not set in England and that it is not an English ruler who is deposed makes no difference whatsoever. Elizabethans had a habit of judging the affairs of other countries by their own national standards. For instance, Brutus and Cassius were regarded as traitors because they dared to rebel against their ruler, Julius Caesar!

Frederick leaves and Celia reaffirms to Rosalind that she, too, considers herself banished and will share her cousin's fortunes. When Rosalind wonders what they should do, it is Celia who comes up with the idea of fleeing to the Forest of Arden to join Rosalind's father. To avoid being molested on the way, decide to disguise themselves. Celia puts on ragged clothes and dirties her face, while Rosalind assumes men's clothing and carries a spear. No matter what woman's fears I may have within me, says Rosalind, at least I shall have an imposing and war-like exterior - and in this respect I will not differ very much from many cowards of the male sex. Along with the change of clothing goes a change of name: Celia takes the name Aliena; Rosalind calls herself Ganymede.

> Comment

Celia's determination to share Rosalind's banishment re-emphasizes their mutual affection and also, in terms of the plot, provides Rosalind with someone in Arden in whom to confide her love for Orlando. The girls disguise themselves for two reasons:

1. Their action complicates the plot and makes possible a series of delicious misunderstandings later on, the most important of which is Orlando's wooing of Ganymede (really Rosalind) as a practice session for wooing Rosalind.

2. Since female parts were played by boy actors (with high voices), the audience, who loved as many complications as possible, were amused at the spectacle of a boy actor pretending to be a girl who is pretending to be a boy.

Rosalind suggests that they take Touchstone along to make them merry on their travels. Celia replies that that will be no problem, as Touchstone is completely devoted to her and will go with her anywhere.

> Comment

The stealing of Touchstone, that critic of society, is purely for the purpose of conveying him to the scene of the forthcoming action in Arden. The fact that Touchstone, one of the most amusing characters in the play, is so fond of Celia, adds to our estimation of his character.

The two girls prepare to set out, Celia with brave and hopeful words on her lips: "Now go we in content / To liberty and not to banishment."

Comment

Celia's concluding **couplet** sets the mood for the opening scene of the following act. These are exactly the sentiments expressed by the banished Duke.

AS YOU LIKE IT

TEXTUAL ANALYSIS

ACT 2

ACT 2: SCENE 1

The scene shifts to the Forest of Arden, where for the first time we meet the banished Duke, or Duke Senior, as he is called. The Duke is extolling the advantages of life in the forest, free from the perils of "the envious Court." He implies that in fact his banishment has been a blessing - "Sweet are the uses of adversity."

Comment

As You Like It was written in a period when two literary fashions were in vogue:

1. Pastoralism, which was the glorification of the supposedly "pure" country over the "wicked" city or court.

2. **Satire** - Elizabethan satire was a criticism of contemporary manners and morals.

In this play Shakespeare combines both vogues by satirizing pastoralism and, as we shall see, by satirizing satirists who criticized merely for the sake of criticism, not reform. The Duke's speech is in the orthodox pastoral vein. Shakespeare pokes fun at this idealized picture of country life in a number of ways to be discussed later.

When the Duke suggests that they hunt deer, an attendant lord mentions that Jaques, one of the Duke's entourage in the forest, objects to the killing of the forest's lawful inhabitants, claiming that in this action the Duke is a greater usurper than his brother. The lord continues that he overheard Jaques moralize at length at the sight of a wounded deer abandoned by his fellows, comparing the plight of the animal to that of a man down on his luck and consequently deserted by his friends.

Comment

Jaques is the self-appointed satirist or critic of the play. His greatest pleasure is in pointing out what he regards as other people's folly. He evidently thinks that his comments are profound (a trait he shares with Polonius in *Hamlet);* actually, they are commonplace.

ACT 2: SCENE 2

In this very short scene, which takes place in Duke Frederick's palace, the angry Duke discovers that Celia and Touchstone have left the Court with Rosalind. Hearing that all three might be with Orlando, he sends for Oliver, intending to make him find his brother and the others.

Comment

The main point of this scene is to motivate Oliver to go to Arden in search of Orlando, so that all the important characters will meet there.

ACT 2: SCENE 3

Orlando, however, is not with Rosalind. He returns to Oliver's house, where he is met at the entrance by a very agitated Adam. The old man laments the fact that Orlando is virtuous, strong, brave, and popular. It would have been much better had Orlando not gained such a victory in the wrestling match, he declares, for praise of him has come to the ears of the wrong people. Orlando is completely at a loss and asks Adam what he means. Adam replies that Oliver has heard Orlando's wrestling feat so highly extolled that, stung with jealousy, he intends to set fire to his youngest brother's room that night and burn him to death. Should this fail, Adam has overheard, Oliver plans to dispose of Orlando in some other way.

Comment

The scene further illustrates the villainy of Oliver, who is evidently prepared to stop at nothing in his attempt to harm his brother. Note that both Oliver and Frederick would fit quite well into a Shakespearean tragedy; they have some of the evil qualities of Claudius in *Hamlet,* Iago in *Othello,* and Edmund in *King Lear.* They do not seem any less clever and they are certainly as ruthless. What makes *As You Like It* a comedy instead of a tragedy is not that it lacks villains, or that its villains are incompetent, or even that the characters say amusing things to each other (they do that too in *Hamlet,* for instance). It is simply that the villains are unsuccessful, so that the fortunes of the main characters (Orlando, Rosalind, Duke Senior) are happier at the end of the play than at the beginning. We are further impressed with the goodness of Orlando for two reasons:

1. He is respected and loved by the common people.

2. He is respected and loved by Adam, an obviously good character. Adam is at the opposite extreme of the scale from Oliver; he is almost a personification of goodness. In between these two extremes of utter evil and utter good come most of the other, more believable characters, such as Orlando and Rosalind.

Orlando is completely at a loss for a hiding place (unlike Rosalind, he has no relatives to flee to in the Forest of Arden), and he is not much helped by Adam's "No matter whither so you come not here." But when he points out that his only alternatives to remaining in his brother's house are to beg or steal, faithful Adam offers his life's savings to his young master, causing the latter to marvel at the kindness of the "good old" world as compared to the cruelty of the present. The two set out into the unknown, convinced that they will be happy, even if poor.

Comment

Both Orlando's praise of the "good old" world and his looking forward to a life of contented poverty anticipate the peaceful mood of the Forest of Arden which Duke Senior expressed in the first scene of this act. Orlando and Adam leave their home in much the same mood as Rosalind and Celia left theirs and Oliver's plot has served to get two more people to the forest, for that is where Adam and Orlando end up.

ACT 2: SCENE 4

Ganymede (Rosalind), Aliena (Celia), and Touchstone arrive in the Forest of Arden. They are all exhausted, and Rosalind complains of the weariness of her spirits. Touchstone says that he cares more about weary legs than weary spirits. Rosalind feels like sitting down and having a good cry, but she remembers that she is supposed to be playing the part of a man and pulls herself together. In her role as a man, she even summons up enough strength to encourage her "female attendant" Aliena, who is almost collapsing and who requests the others, "I pray you bear with me, I cannot go no further." Touchstone thinks that he would much rather "bear with" (be considerate to) Celia than "bear" (carry) her. With a weary sigh, Rosalind looks around and says, "Well, this is the forest of Arden." Touchstone is less than impressed: "When I was at home, I was in a better place," he concludes.

Comment

Touchstone's comments are typical of his practical attitude throughout the play. One of his functions is to serve as a realistic contrast to the romanticism of the other characters. Notice Celia's double negative. Although unacceptable today, it was commonly used for emphasis in Elizabethan English, which was just beginning to develop uniform concepts of grammar and spelling at the time Shakespeare wrote. As explained previously, English was not regarded as important enough a language to have strict grammar and spelling rules. (Shakespeare spelled his own name in many different ways, and Elizabethans were quite capable of spelling the same word repeated three times in succession in three different ways, such as sing, singe, synge.) At the same time, Elizabethans were absolutely consistent in the grammar and spelling of Latin, because Latin had always been recognized as an important language. Incidentally, the spelling in the Shakespeare texts used in high schools and colleges is a modernized spelling for easier reading; Shakespeare's original spelling is quite different.

Rosalind's announcement that they are now in the forest is made more for the benefit of the audience than for Celia and Touchstone. Remember that Shakespeare's stage had no curtain or scenery as we have in the modern theatre. The Elizabethan dramatist had only three ways he could let his audience know where a certain scene was taking place:

1. He could have a sign on which the name of the location was painted.

2. He could have someone come in at the beginning of the scene and announce the location to the audience.

3. He could have one of his characters casually mention the location to another character (or characters) in dialogue.

Shakespeare's characters are always exchanging information which is really not intended so much for the characters they are addressing as for the audience. For instance, at the beginning of this play, Adam would surely already have known everything Orlando told him about Oliver, if Adam had been present in the house all the time, as we are told he was. Adam might really know, but we the audience certainly do not, and it is for our benefit that the conversation takes place. The same is true of the conversation between Oliver and Charles. If Oliver had been living in the Dukedom all the time, how could he possibly not know everything Charles tells him about the two Dukes and their daughters. Oliver knows, but we do not, and again, that conversation is really for our benefit, not Oliver's. The technical term for this means of imparting information to the audience is "exposition." Naturally, a play will have more **exposition** near its beginning, where the audience has to be filled in on facts more frequently than later in the play.

Two shepherds approach - Corin, who is an old man, and a youth, Silvius. Silvius is evidently very much in love with a shepherdess called Phebe, whose name he sighs out mournfully; it seems that he has been wooing Phebe for a long time but that she will have nothing to do with him. When Corin tries to sympathize, Silvius tells him that he cannot possibly understand anything about love because he is an old man.

Comment

Silvius is the typical pastoral lover of Elizabethan romances. He can think of nothing but his love, which causes him loss of sleep and appetite and occupies his thoughts twenty-four hours a day. His name and that of Phebe his mistress (the Elizabethan term for sweetheart), are stock names for lovelorn shepherds and shepherdesses of the pastoral romance, a type of literature in which supposedly simple shepherds engage in sophisticated conversations about love with supposedly simple shepherdesses, while obviously knowing nothing and caring less about their ostensible job, taking care of sheep. The love of

Silvius for Phebe is one of the many varieties of love examined in this play. Through Silvius, Shakespeare is making fun of the pastoral convention.

According to the Elizabethan "Seven Ages" idea, to be expressed later by Jaques in Scene 7, each age has its appropriate activity, and that of a young man is to fall in love. An old man was supposed to be interested only in hoarding money.

On overhearing Silvius' declaration of love for Phebe, Rosalind is reminded of her own love for Orlando. Touchstone, not to be outdone (and perhaps to cheer up Rosalind), remembers a passion (probably imaginary) he once had for a milkmaid. He too, he declares, like Silvius and Rosalind, was completely overcome by love: with his sword he attacked a stone on which his sweetheart had sat, because he was jealous of anyone else or anything else coming near her; he kissed the udders of the cow her hands had milked; and when he could not be with her he wooed a pea plant instead of her: he took two peapods from the plant and then replaced them, saying, with tears, "Wear these for my sake."

Comment

Touchstone satirizes the romantic love of Silvius and Rosalind by telling of his ridiculous love for a milkmaid. Notice that in his wooing of the pea plant, he pokes fun at one thing Rosalind has already done, and at another thing she is yet to do: his giving the plant two peapods as a keepsake is a **parody** of Rosalind's giving her lover her chain. His using the plant as a substitute for his sweetheart is a **parody** of the scheme Rosalind later devises, in which Orlando uses her, dressed as the youth Ganymede, as a substitute for his sweetheart Rosalind.

Meanwhile, Celia (who has no love on which to feed) is almost fainting from hunger. She tells her companions to ask the shepherds if they have any food or know of a place to rest. Corin says he would gladly help them but that he is employed by an inhospitable master, who, in any case, is not at home, because he has put his house and sheep up for sale. On hearing this, the girls decide to buy the house and stock for themselves, employing Corin as shepherd.

Comment

The purchase of the house and sheep provides Rosalind's party with a means of livelihood in the forest. This is a surprising touch of **realism** in an otherwise quite unrealistic play.

ACT 2: SCENE 5

In another part of the forest, Amiens, one of the lords attending Duke Senior, sings a song in praise of pastoral life, "Under the greenwood tree." The song makes the conventional statement of pastoral romances: country life is simple and pure, as opposed to the corruption of city and court life.

Comment

The purpose of the pastoral songs is twofold:

1. They provide music for the play, and the Elizabethan audience was very fond of music.

2. They re-emphasize the rationalization of the courtiers who, along with the Duke, pretend to themselves that "Sweet are the uses of adversity," that is, that banishment is really a boon.

When Amiens stops, Jaques wants to hear more. Told that listening to more songs will make him melancholy, Jaques replies that he loves to be melancholy. He asks Amiens whether the various parts of a song are called stanzas, and when Amiens replies that they can be called anything one likes, Jaques declares that he really is not interested in the subject at all. Amiens excuses himself from singing any more because he knows that he will never please Jaques, to which Jaques replies that he did not ask Amiens to please him, just to sing. Finally Amiens agrees to sing some more, telling Jaques he does it only because Jaques insists, not because he thinks he sings well. To this Jaques replies that he does not care for people who compliment him or thank him. Amiens says that he will end his song and tells Jaques that Duke Senior has been looking for him all day. And I have been trying to avoid him all day, declares Jaques: I find the Duke too argumentative to enjoy his company. Amiens thereupon finishes his song.

Comment

We see Jaques here in his most argumentative vein; he will agree with no one and nothing pleases him. Note that it is he who asks Amiens to tell him about **stanzas** - Amiens does not volunteer the information - and that Jaques then has the gall to say he is not interested in the subject. The most audacious thing, of course, that Jaques says is that the Duke is too argumentative, for no one in the play is as argumentative as Jaques.

When he is finished, Jaques sings a song of his own composition in reply, which says that only fools would leave the ease of the city for the rigors of the country.

Comment

Jaques' song also acts as an antidote to the false sentiment of the pastoral songs. It does not, however, express Jaques' real opinion and was composed and sung only because Jaques cannot help criticizing whatever he hears. (Note that after Jaques has practically forced Amiens to finish the song, he ridicules it.) For Jaques, who pretends to dislike pastoral life as much as the others pretend to like it, is the only one at the end of the play who chooses to remain in the forest, while the others rush back to city and court at the first opportunity.

ACT 2: SCENE 6

Orlando and Adam reach the outskirts of Arden, with Adam exhausted and hungry. Orlando decides to go further into the forest to search for food.

Comment

The purpose of this short scene is to show Orlando's arrival in the forest and to prepare for his meeting with the Duke's party in the next scene.

ACT 2: SCENE 7

In the forest Jaques entertains the Duke and his followers with an account of his meeting with Touchstone (in spite of the fact that he has just told us he cannot stand the Duke).

Comment

Despite Jaques' dislike for the Duke - actually he does not really get along with anyone in the play - he needs the Duke or anyone else who will listen to him so he can hold forth on what he calls his philosophy. The consequence of Jaques' argumentative and critical nature is that no one really likes him or cares to spend one moment longer in his company than necessary.

Jaques is full of admiration for Touchstone, because he thinks that in the jester he has found a kindred spirit. He is impressed by the fact that Touchstone "railed on Lady Fortune" (criticized life generally). But what he admires most about Touchstone is what Jaques considers Touchstone's philosophical observations on life. Jaques reports that Touchstone took a watch from his pocket, looked at it dully, and proclaimed that it was ten o'clock. Touchstone continued by saying that only one hour ago it was nine, and in another hour it would be eleven, whereupon he concluded that "from hour to hour, we ripe and ripe,/ And then from hour to hour, we rot and rot ...." Well, says Jaques, when I heard this man, evidently a fool by his multicolored clothes, thus philosophize on the passage of time in such a deep fashion, I began to laugh heartily for one whole hour, for I timed myself by Touchstone's watch.

Comment

Touchstone has obviously taken Jaques' measure - as Touchstone takes the measure of everybody in the play - and is getting a rise out of Jaques. For what Jaques regards at profound thinking is ridiculously shallow stuff. But since Touchstone's **clichés** are of the kind Jaques himself inflicts on others, he takes them as a sign of Touchstone's wisdom. Touchstone is wise, in fact, but not for what he says to Jaques.

Touchstone's watch is peculiarly inappropriate in a forest where most people "Lose and neglect the creeping hours of time." It is a sign that he, at least, is not out of touch with the real world; the forest has not enchanted him. But Jaques' use of the watch, to time himself to laugh exactly one hour, does not show Jaques' keeping in touch with reality but rather how artificial and ridiculous a person he really is; genuine laughter, surely cannot be timed or turned on and off like a faucet.

So impressed is Jaques by Touchstone and his profession, that he expresses a desire to become a licensed fool too, so that he might criticize whomever he wished without fear of retaliation.

Comment

Since the court fool was by **convention** regarded as mad, no person wishing to be regarded as sane would take offense at anything he said. Thus the official or licensed fool at court could insult anyone he pleased, including his own master; in the household of a powerful man, the licensed fool was usually the only one at liberty to tell his master the truth instead of flattering him. Very often in Shakespeare's plays the fool is actually one of the sanest persons (notably in *King Lear*), and this is certainly the case in *As You Like It*.

The Duke says that Jaques is the last person who should take it upon himself to criticize the morals of society, for he, at one time or another, has practiced most of its vices and he would be more likely to infect the world than cure it. Oh no, replies Jaques, he would do only good, because only the guilty would be hurt by his attacks, since his **satire** would be general rather than particular; that is, he would not mention anyone by name. In this way the innocent would not feel that they were included in Jaques' exposures of sin and vice, while those who were offended would, by the very fact that they were offended, prove themselves guilty.

Comment

The Duke's revelation that Jaques himself has practiced many of the vices and follies he wants to satirize further illuminates Jaques' character; he is a hypocrite as well as a bore. Just as the extravagant pastoralism of Silvius is intended to satirize the absurdities of the late sixteenth-century pastoral **convention**, so the repeated exposure of the shortcomings of the professional satirist Jaques is intended to demonstrate some of the absurdities of late sixteenth-century **satire**; contemporary satirists were always saying what Jaques says here - that only those who are guilty of the vice or folly satirized will object to their **satire** - a very convenient way to prevent criticism of their activity.

Jaques is interrupted by Orlando, who bursts in on the party with drawn sword and demands food. Jaques behaves very coolly in the face of danger. To Orlando's "Forbear, and eat no more," the professional critic Jaques corrects the intruder's statement by saying "Why, I have eat none yet." The Duke (less interested than Jaques in correct forms of speech) asks Orlando whether he has been made to consider robbery by dire necessity, or whether he just naturally despises the laws of ordered society. Orlando replies that the former is his case; he has been well brought up (something of a contradiction to what he says at the beginning of the play) but that circumstances have made him desperate. Orlando is very surprised when the Duke tells him that he is welcome to some food, and that he does not have to demand it at sword-point. "I thought that all things had been savage here," exclaims Orlando, and therefore I was so aggressive. But, he says to the Duke and his followers, I see that you are gentlemen. Whoever you are who in this forest "Lose and neglect the creeping hours of time," if you have ever looked on better days, if you have ever gone to church, if you have ever sat at a good man's table, if you have ever had to wipe a tear from your eyes and know what pity is, forgive me for what I have done and help me. We have experienced all these things you describe, the Duke tells Orlando, and therefore we will try to help you. Orlando thanks him for his kindness and explains that he has left Adam in another part of the forest. He goes to fetch him when the Duke assures him that both are welcome.

Comment

The fact that Orlando says here that he has been well brought up, but at the beginning of the play complains of the opposite, should not shock or surprise us. In Shakespeare's day, plays were regarded much as television scripts are today, not as "literature," and Shakespeare wrote his plays at tremendous speed. Thus there are many inconsistencies in his plays, as well as many factual errors. For instance, at the beginning of this play Shakespeare tells us that Celia is taller than Rosalind, but later refers to Rosalind as being taller than Celia. If you note the animal life in the Forest of Arden - presumably the Ardennes Forest in Belgium - you will realize that in no forest in the world do lions, snakes, and sheep live together, and that there were certainly no lions in sixteenth-century Belgium. Those who think that Shakespeare's works are filled with superhuman wisdom and that Shakespeare never made a mistake do him no service; Shakespeare's contemporary, Ben Jonson, thought he made many. It was partly from the overestimation of the wisdom contained in Shakespeare's works that the notion arose that so supposedly uneducated a man as Shakespeare of Stratford could not possibly have written them.

Referring to the plight of Orlando and Adam, the Duke turns to Jaques and tells him, "Thou seest we are not alone unhappy," and that in this great theatre of the world there are many people worse off than they.

Comment

The Duke's remark to Jaques is very revealing, for it is an inadvertent admission that, contrary to what he has previously said, he is not really happy in Arden.

The Duke's remark causes Jaques to launch into his "Seven Ages of Man" speech, in which (using the **imagery** of the theatre) he describes the world as a stage, the seven divisions of man's life from birth to death as the seven acts of a play, and man himself as an actor. Just as actors have their exits and entrances, says Jaques, and in the course of their careers, play many different parts, so do men. First there is the part of the infant, whimpering and vomiting, held in his nurse's arms. Then there is the reluctant schoolboy, with his books and his face newly scrubbed clean so that it shines, creeping unwillingly to school at a snail's pace, really not wanting to go at all. Then, when the schoolboy has grown up to be a young man, he begins to play the part of a lover, sighing out his love for his sweetheart with a noise like the bellows of a furnace, and writing endless love poems to win her favor. A little older and the young man becomes a soldier, full of new oaths learned in camp and battlefield, heavily bearded, and concerned about his reputation for courage. He is quick to quarrel with any man from whom he even suspects an insult, and seeks fame, which will last as long as will a bubble, by storming right up to the mouth of the enemy cannon. Having survived the war, the soldier returns to civilian life and becomes a judge in his home town. He becomes fat with bribes brought to him by petitioners and claimants. He assumes a judicial air and dresses to command respect, and now, in place of oaths, his speech is seasoned with proverbs and wise sayings. After this he begins to become senile. He now has to wear spectacles and has lost so much of the weight gained as a judge that his clothes are much too big for him. Even his voice has deserted him or, rather, it has returned to the same pitch it had when he was a child. Last of all, he returns completely to childishness: his powers of reasoning and memory have gone, not to speak of his teeth and eyesight. Thus ends this strange play called life.

Comment

Jaques' "Seven Ages" speech is typical of him on two counts:

1. It is not nearly so profound as he obviously thinks it is.

2. It criticizes each of the seven ages; not one is depicted as pleasant.

Orlando returns with Adam, and the scene ends with another song sung by Amiens in praise of pastoral life, "Blow, blow, thou winter wind," during which Orlando reveals his parentage to the Duke and is welcomed as the son of an old friend.

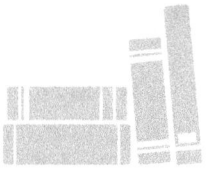

AS YOU LIKE IT

TEXTUAL ANALYSIS

ACT 3

ACT 3: SCENE 1

Meanwhile, Duke Frederick has summoned Oliver to his palace to ask him the whereabouts of Orlando, whom he believes to be with his daughter Celia and Rosalind. He is furious when Oliver does not know. Oliver is told that if he does not bring his brother back within a year, dead or alive, he will be banished from the Duke's territory and his lands will be forfeit. When Oliver tells the Duke he will be happy to obey his commands since he has always hated his brother, the Duke retorts, "More villain thou."

Comment

This scene completes the action begun in Act 2, Scene 2. Its purpose is to motivate Oliver to set out for Arden, so that he might be brought into contact with the other characters already there. The Duke's comment to Oliver is an ironic comment on himself, for he too has hated his brother.

ACT 3: SCENE 2

Orlando enters with a paper on which he has written a love poem to Rosalind. He calls upon Diana, goddess of the moon and of chastity, to witness his love for the chaste Rosalind, whose name he intends to carve on all the trees of the forest. He exits, and Corin enters in conversation with Touchstone. Corin asks him how he likes a shepherd's life. Touchstone replies (with characteristic **realism** and wit) that in itself a shepherd's life is a good life, but that insofar as it is a shepherd's life, it is worthless. "In respect that it is solitary," says Touchstone, he likes it very well, "but in respect that it is private [solitary]," he does not like it at all. Inasmuch as it is in the fields, thinks Touchstone, it pleases him very much, but inasmuch as it is not in the Court, he finds it tedious. He concludes by saying that as it is a life of frugality, it suits his disposition, but as there is not more abundance in it, it goes against his grain. Then he turns to Corin and asks, "Hast any philosophy in thee, shepherd?"

Corin answers that his knowledge of philosophy extends no further than knowing that sickness is unpleasant, that it is good to have money and happiness, that rain wets and fire burns, and that the cause of darkness is the lack of light. Touchstone asks Corin whether he has ever been to Court, and when the shepherd says he has not, Touchstone declares that then he must be damned and go to hell. Corin cannot understand this, and Touchstone explains that if he has never been to Court he has never seen good manners ("good" here bears the double meaning of "morally good" and "socially acceptable"); if he has never seen good manners, then his manners must be wicked (that is, he must be an immoral person); wickedness is a sin, and the penalty for sin is damnation. Touchstone concludes by warning Corin that he is in a very dangerous situation. Corin disagrees and tries to defend himself by pointing out that what are regarded as good manners at Court are not necessarily good manners in the country. For instance, he says, at Court it is the custom to kiss hands on meeting, but for shepherds, whose hands are dirty from handling sheep, this custom would be ridiculous. But Touchstone will not allow Corin's argument; courtiers' hands get just as dirty from sweating, he claims, as do shepherds' from working, and he challenges Corin to produce better proof that he is not bound for eternal damnation. Corin advances several other reasons why Court manners are out of place in the country, but Touchstone mockingly dismisses each of his arguments, so that in the end Corin gives up, saying to his opponent, "You have too Courtly a wit for me, I'll rest." At this the irrepressible Touchstone exclaims, "Wilt thou rest damned? God help thee, shallow man!"

Comment

In contrast to Silvius, the idealized shepherd of pastoral convention, who knows much about the language of love and nothing about keeping sheep, Corin is a real shepherd, who obviously knows something about sheep and little about anything else. He certainly fails to see that Touchstone is making fun of him by using doubletalk, in that he constantly contradicts himself through the use of synonyms beyond Corin's vocabulary, such as "private" and "solitary." Nor does Corin see the joke when, after spouting gibberish, Touchstone asks him if he has any deep philosophy of his own to add to what has already been said. The simple ideas Corin does offer as wisdom are really no less profound than most of Jaques' contributions, and this is something Corin and Jaques have in common; they are both not very bright. Corin was put in the play to demonstrate how real shepherds think and talk; through him we see how unreal a shepherd Silvius is. Thus, Corin is part of the attack on pastoralism.

The two are interrupted by Rosalind, who enters a love poem. (It is one of those written by Orlando, and it is conventionally extravagant in the fashion of the period): "From the east to western Ind [India],/ No jewel is like Rosalind. Her worth, being mounted on the wind [taken up and scattered abroad by the wind],/ Through all the world bears Rosalind./ All the pictures fairest lined [drawn]/ Are but black to Rosalind...."

Comment

Note that in Orlando's poem the words "wind" and "lined" **rhyme**. This means that in Shakespeare's day, either the word "lined" was pronounced as is the modern "sinned," or "wind" was pronounced as is the modern "kind." The only way to settle the question is to observe how "lined" and "wind" rime with other words whose pronunciation we have already established. In Act 2, Scene 7, Amiens sing: "Blow, blow, thou winter wind./ Thou art not so unkind/ As man's ingratitude...." Here "wind" rimes with "unkind." From this and from similar evidence, we can conclude that in Shakespeare's day "wind" was pronounced as is the modern "kind." The method just illustrated is the method used to arrive at the pronunciation of all of Shakespeare's words.

Touchstone is not impressed by the quality of the poetry and claims he could write continuously for eight years in that style, "dinners and suppers and sleeping hours excepted" (he hastens to add in his realistic fashion). To prove that his is no idle boast, he then and there rattles off a poem in the same meter as the love poem (but which satirizes rather than compliments Rosalind): "If a hart [male deer] do lack a hind [female deer],/ Let him seek out Rosalind./ If the cat will after kind,/ So be sure will Rosalind...."

Comment

Touchstone's **realism**, which always concerns itself with practical matters the other characters tend to forget, such as eating and sleeping, is here brought to bear on Orlando's idealization of Rosalind. Love poems not much better than Orlando's were being produced in vast quantities at the time this play was written, and here Shakespeare brings them under attack.

Celia enters reading another poem in praise of Rosalind, and the two cousins decide it is time to confer privately about this strange new development, and so ask Corin and Touchstone to leave them alone.

When Celia asks Rosalind whether she knows who might be writing verses in her praise, Rosalind replies that she has no idea. It is obvious that Celia does know who the poet is, and she teases the, by now, very impatient Rosalind by alternately giving her clues and allowing herself to be sidetracked. Finally she reveals the news that it is Orlando. This revelation completely flusters Rosalind, so that she subjects Celia to a barrage of questions, all of which she wants answered immediately: "What shall I do with my doublet and hose her [male attire]? What did he when thou sawest him? What said he? How looked he? Wherein went he? What makes he here? Did he ask for me? Where remains he? How parted he with thee? And when shalt thou see him again?" We can sympathize with Celia, who answers that she would need the mouth of a giant to answer all these questions at once. She tries to answer Rosalind's questions, but Rosalind is too excited to listen and keeps interrupting Celia's account of where she saw Orlando with comments on each particular piece of information.

Comment

One of the best incidental touches in the play is Rosalind's reaction to hearing that Orlando is in the forest - her dismay that he will see her in man's clothing, her fear that he will not think her beautiful. What she forgets, of course, in her excitement, is that just because of her disguise Orlando will not know that it is Rosalind he is looking at.

Orlando and Jaques enter, and the two girls hide themselves to overhear the conversation. The men have evidently quarreled over Orlando's carving love poems on the barks of trees. Jaques tells Orlando that he is a fool for falling in love and that, as a matter of fact, he was just looking for a fool when he found him. Orlando tells Jaques that he should look in a brook and there he would find his fool, to which Jaques naively answers that there he would see only his own face. Just so, says Orlando, whereupon Jaques leaves him.

Comment

Since Jaques is critical of everything and everybody, he gets along with nobody. Least of all will he approve of lovers and love; like Malvolio in *Twelfth Night* and Polonius in *Hamlet,* he is too much in love with himself. His stupidity is brought out nowhere so clearly as here, when he acts as "straight man" to Orlando's hoary joke about looking at yourself in a mirror and seeing a fool.

Rosalind, still dressed as a man, comes out of her hiding place and engages Orlando in conversation, which she skillfully steers around to the subject of love. She mentions that she was educated by her uncle who, among other things, taught her a cure for love. She wishes she could meet the man who has been carving Rosalind on all the trees, for that man seems to be sadly in need of her cure. When Orlando tells her that he is the man, Rosalind pretends not to believe him, for he has none of the conventional marks of the lover, such as the haggard face, the black marks under the eyes from lack of sleep, the glum appearance, the neglected beard and disordered clothing. When Orlando swears that nevertheless he is very much in love, Rosalind hits on a happy idea of how to cure him of his love and thus relieve him of his misery. If Orlando will pretend that she is Rosalind and come every day to woo her, she, pretending to be his mistress, Rosalind, will act so unreasonably and changeably - as women do - that he will forswear women for the rest of his life. To this Orlando agrees.

Comment

The agreement between Rosalind and Orlando prepares for the most delightful and humorous part of the play, which has all the complications the Elizabethans loved - Rosalind, disguised as Ganymede, will pretend to Orlando that she is only pretending to be Rosalind for the sake of curing him of his love. Rosalind's description of how a lover should look was the conventional medieval and Renaissance conception, personified by Silvius in this play. This love **convention** had as its basis the assumption that the lady was nobler and purer than her lover. Therefore, he had to prove himself worthy of her love. Until he did this, she would reject his advances. This conventional idea was the motivating force behind most of the adventures of the medieval knight; it was to prove himself worthy of his lady's love that he rode away for a year and a day to rid the country of dragons and evil knights. During the Renaissance (presumably because all the dragons had been killed) the lover wrote love poems to his lady, telling how much his love for her was making him suffer. In this manner he tried to purify himself through suffering, arouse the lady's pity, and make himself worthy of her love. This love relationship (sometimes called Petrarchan love because it was celebrated by Petrarch in his love **sonnets** to his lady Laura) is one of the number of **conventions** satirized in this play.

ACT 3: SCENE 3

Touchstone has met Audrey, a country wench, whom he is wooing vigorously. He is somewhat hampered by the fact that Audrey usually does not have the faintest idea what he means when he is talking to her. Her vocabulary is even more limited than Corin's. When Touchstone asks her whether she likes his feature, meaning his appearance, she fails to understand him, and when her lover wishes the gods had made her poetical, she confesses her ignorance of that word too. Her own handling of language is no better than her comprehension, so that she innocently says, "I thank the gods I am foul," which in Elizabethan English meant "ugly."

> Comment

Audrey, like Corin, is a real country figure, and her function in the play, like his, is to demonstrate that country people, especially shepherds and shepherdesses, are not all like Silvius and his love, Phebe, whom we are to meet later. Particularly, real country people do not talk like Silvius and Phebe and all the other highly articulate pastoral figures of the conventional romance. It is to underscore this point that so much is made of the inability of Corin and Audrey to express themselves.

When Jaques, who has witnessed Touchstone's strange wooing, expresses amazement that one of Touchstone's breeding would marry someone like Audrey, Touchstone explains that what motivates him is not love but sexual desire. In fact, he sees some advantage to being married by an incompetent, appropriately called Sir Oliver Martext, on the assumption that a marriage ceremony performed by such a man will be bound to have mistakes in it and therefore not be binding: "... it will be a good excuse for me hereafter to leave my wife," thinks Touchstone. However, on the advice of Jaques, the wedding is postponed.

> Comment

Touchstone's sexual love for Audrey stands in contrast to the romantic love of Silvius for Phebe and of Orlando for Rosalind. The purpose of the Touchstone-Audrey relationship is not to attack all romantic love, but just its more ridiculous features, such as those Silvius always, and Orlando occasionally, exhibits.

ACT 3: SCENE 4

Rosalind is impatiently awaiting the arrival of Orlando, who is supposed to receive his first lesson in curing love. He is late, and Rosalind, who fears Orlando might be late because he is no longer in love, is at the point of tears. In her frustration she begins to criticize Orlando, but as soon as Celia sympathetically joins in on the criticism, she vehemently defends Orlando in every respect; she can criticize him, but no one else can. Celia, however, proceeds with a very cool examination of Orlando and concludes that he is more of a talker than a doer, that he writes and speaks feelingly about love, but fails when it comes to doing anything about it. She confirms Rosalind's own fears by concluding that Orlando may have been in love, but is not any more.

Comment

We see here just how deeply in love Rosalind is. Celia, partly because she is not yet in love herself, and partly because of her own nature, is always more cool and level-headed than her cousin.

As this point Corin enters and invites the girls to watch the spectacle of Silvius vainly wooing the proud Phebe.

Comment

Corin's invitation serves as a link to the next scene and as a preparation for it. Shakespeare very rarely presents a scene for which he has not prepared his audience. He usually tries to have the audience come to a scene already predisposed to laugh or cry, to be frightened or delighted, so that the subsequent action will have greater effect.

ACT 3: SCENE 5

Silvius feels so unworthy in the presence of his lady Phebe, and she has rejected him so often, that he does not dare beg for her love anymore; he merely implores her not to hate him. Phebe replies that she does not hate him, and certainly has no intention of being the cause of his death, as Silvius has often claimed she would be if she did not take pity on him. But she does not love him. She also does not believe that her eyes have in them the power to kill, as Silvius claims. Frowning on him severely, she asks him to show her the wound her eyes have made. Silvius replies that should Phebe ever fall in love, she will "know the wounds invisible/ That love's keen arrows make." To this Phebe replies that she is content to wait until that time comes, if ever, and that in the meantime she wants Silvius to get out of her sight.

Comment

We have previously only heard about Silvius' great passion for Phebe; now we see it demonstrated. The scene is a **satire** on the conventional love situation; Silvius feels he is completely unworthy of his lady's love but, hoping against hope, he persists in wooing her. The lady coldly rejects all his advances and ridicules his sufferings. She (and presumably Shakespeare) is tired of hearing the language of conventional love, in which the lover swears he will die if his lady frowns on him.

Rosalind, who has been listening to Phebe abuse true love, can stand it no longer and bursts out of her hiding place, followed by Celia and Corin. She turns on Phebe and demands to know why Phebe dares treat Silvius so. Just because you are ugly, she asks, is this a reason to be proud and devoid of pity? Rosalind continues by itemizing Phebe's defects, telling Silvius that he is much handsomer than Phebe is beautiful, so that she really cannot understand why he bothers with her. She advises Phebe to accept Silvius quickly, as, with her looks, she might never get another offer.

Comment

Rosalind objects to Phebe's harsh treatment of her lover because she herself is in love. This does not mean that she approves of the artificiality of the Petrarchan love **convention**; she does not, as we learn later. She just does not want to see any lover abused, no matter how foolish he may be.

While she has been berating Phebe, Rosalind, who, we must remember, is dressed as a man, has noticed Phebe eyeing her intently. She concludes that Phebe must have fallen in love with her, and this is immediately confirmed by Phebe's first words, "Sweet youth, I pray you, chide a year together/I had rather hear you chide than this man woo." Rosalind warns Phebe against falling in love with her and leaves, along with Celia and Corin.

Comment

Phebe's falling in love with Rosalind disguised as Ganymede is another instance of Shakespeare's catering to the Elizabethan taste for complication. (The same thing happens in *Twelfth Night*, where Olivia falls in love with Viola, who is disguised as a man.) We now have a variety of love situations in the play:

Orlando's permissibly romantic love for Rosalind (permissible in the sense that both, and especially Rosalind, keep their feet on the ground - their love does not make them foolish); Silvius' excessively romantic love for Phebe; Phebe's misplaced love for Rosalind; and Touchstone's completely unromantic (sexual) love for Audrey.

Left alone with Silvius, the love-smitten Phebe finds that she now likes his company, not because she loves or even likes him for himself, but because he can "talk of love so well," and she hits on a plan of using him. She warns Silvius not to "look for further recompense/ Than thine own gladness that thou art employed." Emphasizing to Silvius that she is not in love with Rosalind, but revealing to the audience by her remarks that she is completely infatuated, she commissions Silvius to carry what she calls "a very taunting letter" to Rosalind.

Comment

The only reason Silvius cannot see that Phebe is in love with Rosalind is that whatever wits he may have had have been scattered by his great love.

AS YOU LIKE IT

TEXTUAL ANALYSIS

ACT 4

ACT 4: SCENE 1

Jaques meets Rosalind in the forest and expresses a desire to become acquainted with her. Rosalind has heard that Jaques has a reputation for being melancholy and asks him if what she has heard is true. When Jaques answers that he loves melancholy rather than laughter, Rosalind answers that any extreme, whether of sadness or of gaiety, is to be avoided. To Jaques' reply that "'tis good to be sad and say nothing," Rosalind counters, "Why, then 'tis good to be a post."

Comment

Jaques, the self-appointed critic of society, comes off badly in his meeting with all the other principal characters of the play. We have already seen how he has been made a fool of by Touchstone and Orlando; now it is the turn of Rosalind to satirize the satirist.

Rosalind's denunciation of going to extremes is one of the points of the play. There is nothing wrong with romantic love, so long as it does not make lovers into complete fools. That is why the love of Orlando and Rosalind does not appear ridiculous, while the love of Silvius for Phebe does. The first pair, especially Rosalind, behave in love the way they really feel like behaving, whereas Silvius does not act naturally but in accordance with an established love **convention**. The idea that extremes tend to be ridiculous is also true in matters other than love. There is nothing wrong with criticizing society; it can usually stand criticism. But there is something wrong with a character like Jaques who has become a "professional" critic, spending his entire life criticizing, and seeing no good in anything. The idea that the middle way was usually the best was a popular one when this play was written; it was an important feature in the plays of Shakespeare's contemporary, Ben Jonson.

Jaques now launches into a description of his melancholy which, he claims, is unlike that of any other person; he concludes that his extensive travels have made him sad. Rosalind cannot see the advantage of spending money for foreign travel if the result is to make the traveler sad; perhaps with Touchstone in mind, she concludes that she would rather have a fool to make her merry. Orlando enters and greets Rosalind elaborately, whereupon Jaques, who remembers how Orlando made a fool of him in their last meeting, hastily withdraws. Rosalind bids him farewell and sarcastically reminds him to act like the typical Englishman who has returned to his native country after having traveled abroad: to affect a foreign accent and foreign clothing, to criticize his own country, and to bemoan the fact that he was born an Englishman.

Comment

To be or to pretend to be melancholy was very fashionable at the turn of the sixteenth century. This may seem a strange fashion today, but our fashions will seem just as strange to succeeding centuries. Jaques' melancholy is associated with his being a traveler. The English traveler who returned to his own country only to run it down was a favorite butt of **satire** among the Elizabethans. He is comparable to the American who has been to Europe and who returns to find nothing good in his own land, who wears only English clothes, if a man, or only French clothes, if a woman, who affects an English accent and sprinkles it with choice French and Italian phrases. Such a sixteenth-century Englishman was a source of **satire** for two reasons:

1. The great number of gentlemen and would-be gentlemen who did travel abroad. England was not yet thought of as having much culture of her own at this time, and if one wanted to become more polished one went abroad - to France, and especially to Italy.

2. The growing nationalism of the English. More and more European nations were thinking of themselves as distinct units; they no longer thought of themselves merely as Christians, as they had done during the Middle Ages, but as Frenchmen, Spaniards, and Englishmen. This feeling of national pride was increased in England after the defeat of the Spanish Armada in 1588. So naturally, Englishmen resented those compatriots who came back from abroad only to criticize their own country.

Rosalind turns on Orlando and chides him for being late. He certainly does not act like a lover, she thinks, and warns him that if he is ever late again she will not see him anymore.

When Orlando protests that he is only one hour late, Rosalind becomes furious and demands to know how anyone in love can consider an hour's lateness for a tryst to be a trifle. No one, she says, who can be late even a fraction of a minute in an affair of love deserves the name of a true lover. She would rather be wooed by a snail, she concludes, than by a tardy lover, for a snail, although slow, carries his house about with him, so that his wife will not have to look for a place to live; besides, the snail already has horns, saving his wife the trouble of providing him with a pair. To this Orlando answers that when the lady is virtuous the lover will never wear horns, and that his Rosalind is virtuous he knows for certain. At this, Rosalind is evidently so pleased that she almost gives the whole show away, for she says, "And I am your Rosalind." Celia intervenes just in time by saying that of course they are only pretending that Ganymede is Rosalind for the sake of curing Orlando of his love.

Comment

The comedy in the wooing of Ganymede (Rosalind) by Orlando derives from a number of sources:

1. The complicated situation. Orlando thinks he is pretending to woo his lady, while in reality he is actually doing so.

2. The number of times Rosalind, in her delight at hearing herself praised by her lover, nearly gives herself away.

3. Rosalind's obvious enjoyment of the situation. Because of her disguise she need not play the conventional part of the shy girl; she can say all the things she would like to say to her lover without appearing immodest.

Horns on a man's head were the traditional sign of the cuckold, a man deceived by his wife. Jokes about horns appear often in Shakespeare's plays.

Rosalind, still delighted by what Orlando had said about her, gaily instructs him to woo her, for she is in such a good mood that she will probably accept him. Realizing that once again she has allowed herself to be carried away and to forget that she is supposed to be playing a part, she draws herself up and asks Orlando what he would say to her now if she really were his Rosalind. Before I said anything I would kiss her, says Orlando. Rosalind does not think that is a very good approach. Much better, she says, to speak first, and when you have run out of things to say and are trying to think of new material, you should kiss. Yes, says Orlando, but what if she will not let me kiss her? No problem there, says Rosalind, for her denial will give you something else to say; you will plead with her to let you.

Comment

In coaching Orlando how to woo, Rosalind describes the force which caused so many love **sonnets** to be written in Shakespeare's day. These poems all rest on the conventional rejection of the lover by the conventionally aloof lady; their stated purpose is to get the lady to have pity on the miserable lover and accept him.

Now, says Rosalind, suddenly shifting tactics, as Rosalind's stand-in I say I will not accept you. Then I shall die, Orlando exclaims. Oh, I don't think so, Rosalind says coolly. The world is almost six-thousand years old, and in all that time not a single man has ever died for love. Even such legendary lovers as Troilus, in love with Cressida, or Leander, in love with Hero, died for reasons other than love. "Men have died from time to time and worms have eaten them, but not for love," Rosalind concludes. When Orlando says he would not like his real Rosalind to have such an opinion, for he thinks that even her frown would kill him, Rosalind raises her hand and says, "By this hand, it will not kill a fly."

Comment

Rosalind's assertion that no man has ever really died of love is the classic instance in this play of Shakespeare's satiric treatment of Petrarchan love. We have already noted Silvius' claim that Phebe's frown would kill him - Orlando says the same thing to Rosalind here - and such a claim, typical of the Petrarchan love poem, is here ridiculed. Rosalind's scoffing in this play. Dramatic **irony** occurs when the audience is in post the power of her frown is a beautiful instance of dramatic **irony** session of more facts than one (or a number) of the characters. In this case the audience knows that Ganymede is really Rosalind (a fact that Orlando does not know), and that Ganymede's statements about Rosalind are not mere opinion. The entire situation of the disguise, of course, is one of dramatic irony.

Rosalind's mood changes again, and she promises Orlando that she will grant anything he asks. He proposes, is accepted, and Celia, officiating in place of a priest, marries Orlando and Rosalind in a mock marriage ceremony. When Orlando swears that he will be faithful to his real Rosalind forever, Rosalind laughs at him and says that both men and women behave quite differently after they are married. Orlando thinks his Rosalind would never behave badly, to which Rosalind replies, "By my life, she will do as I do." Orlando protests that his Rosalind is wise, which prompts Rosalind to say, "Or else she could not have the wit to do this" (referring to the arrangement she has set up, whereby Orlando woos her thinking she is only pretending to be Rosalind).

Orlando tells Rosalind that he must leave her for two hours and that he will be with her again at two o'clock. Rosalind is reluctant to let him go at all and makes him swear that this time he will not be even one minute late. Upon this, Orlando leaves and Rosalind confesses to Celia how deeply in love she is.

ACT 4: SCENE 2

Jaques enters with some lords and foresters who have just killed a deer. Jaques sneeringly suggests that the deer be presented to the Duke in the form of a trophy of great victory, as captives were presented to victorious Roman emperors. Ironically, he asks one of the foresters if he does not have a song to celebrate this great occasion, adding (in his characteristically bitter fashion), "'Tis no matter how it be in tune so it make noise enough."

Comment

We once again see Jaques in his usual role of critic. The scene is a sequel to Act 2, Scene, 1, in which Jaques was reported as objecting to the Duke's killing deer in the forest. Note that here again we have the typically Shakespearean technique of first reporting an incident or attitude and then dramatizing it.

The forester sings a song which discusses what reward would be most suitable for the man who killed the deer. The answer is that he should be given the horns to wear, and the entire company joins in the chorus: "Take thou no scorn to wear the horn,/ It was a crest ere thou wast born./ Thy father's father wore it...."

Comment

The song about the deer has as its point the usual joke about cuckoldry, of which the symbol was a pair of horns growing out of the deceived husband's forehead. A wife who was unfaithful to her husband was said to have presented him with a pair of horns. Shakespeare's plays are full of jokes not only about adultery but about sex in general, often quite crudely expressed. This can be attributed to:

1. The general taste of the age.

2. The particular nature of Shakespeare's audience.

Elizabethans generally expressed themselves much more freely than is considered good taste today. Elizabeth herself, for instance, was famous for her swearing ability. The roughness of Elizabethan language mirrors the roughness of the age, The heads of traitors were displayed in public places as a warning to others. People who came to watch Shakespeare's plays in the afternoon (two o'clock was the usual starting time) might have enjoyed themselves in the morning watching a pack of dogs baiting a bear at the nearby Beargarden.

Although many people have been amazed at what they consider a great amount of knowledge and wisdom displayed in Shakespeare's plays (these are usually people not acquainted with the age in which Shakespeare lived), these plays were not regarded as "highbrow" by his contemporaries. Such plays were being written at the time for the "off-Broadway" theatre of Shakespeare's day, but Shakespeare's plays were definitely "Broadway." They were written for a mass audience and they were successful. Shakespeare was the most popular dramatist of his day; everybody went to see his plays, including all levels of society. To keep such an audience happy, Shakespeare had to have something for everybody. That is one of the reasons there is so much **burlesque** (very often with sexual overtones) in Shakespeare mixed in with the philosophic soliloquies of *Hamlet*. He had to please all parts of his audience, from the man who did not even know how to read to the sophisticated scholar.

ACT 4: SCENE 3

Rosalind and Celia are awaiting the arrival of Orlando for another lesson. Orlando is late. Celia teases Rosalind by saying that Orlando is probably so much in love that he has gone to sleep and forgotten all about his appointment. Silvius enters bearing a letter from Phebe to Rosalind. He says that he does not know what is in the letter, but, judging from how angry Phebe looked when she was writing it, he is sure its contents are not very pleasant. Rosalind looks at the letter and tells Silvius that what it says is so provoking as to be unbearable: Phebe said Rasalind was ugly, lacked manners, was proud, and that she would not fall in love with Rosalind were she the last man on earth. Rosalind angrily turns on Silvius and says Phebe could not have written this, no woman could have written it; the letter is too cutting and cruel to have come from a woman, and she accuses Silvius of having written the letter himself. Silvius protests that he certainly did not write the letter, that Phebe did. Rosalind proceeds to read the letter aloud, commenting on passages as she goes along. The letter opens: "Why, thy godhead laid apart (why did you lay aside your divinity and attack. She continues to read: "Whiles the eye of man did woo me,/ become a man), Warr'st thou with a woman's heart? On this Rosalind comments to Silvius that never in her life has she heard such a vicious That could do no vengeance to me." The meaning of these lines is, of course, clear, Rosalind declares; Phebe means that I am no human but an animal. She goes go with the rhymed letter, which quite unmistakably declares Phebe's love for Rosalind, until even Silvius sees that Phebe has taken advantage of him. Celia is sorry for Silvius, but Rosalind thinks he deserves no pity if he loves such a woman as Phebe.

Comment

Rosalind, at first, is obviously not reporting what is really in the letter but is trying to spare Silvius' feelings by pretending that it contains the kind of material Phebe said it did. Her accusation that Silvius has written the letter instead of Phebe is part of this pretense. The question then arises - why, if Rosalind does not want Silvius to know that the woman he loves has employed him to carry a love letter to another man (Ganymede), does she read the letter aloud? There are a number of possible answers:

1. Rosalind must read the letter aloud on some occasion if the audience is to know what it says. Still, she could have waited until Silvius was no longer present or she could have taken Celia aside and read it only to her.

2. Rosalind may have thought that even will she read the letter to Silvius, predisposed as he was to think the letter an angry one, he still would not understand that it was really a love letter. Her attempts to misinterpret the letter as she reads it lend some support to this theory. Then, when she finds that Silvius is not deceived by her interpretation, she gives up her attempts at deception.

3. Shakespeare may not have noted the inconsistency in Rosalind's actions.

Of the three, the second answer is the most likely.

Rosalind tells Sivius to return to Phebe and inform her that if she loves Ganymede, Ganymede commands her to love Silvius. If she will not do this, Rosalind says she will have nothing more to do with her.

Comment

Rosalind's command must have sounded peculiar to Phebe, accustomed as she was to the **conventions** of pastoral love. According to the medieval convention of love inherited by the Renaissance romance, the lover must do whatever his mistress commands him. One of the problems involved in such a situation: if your mistress commands you to stop loving her, should you obey? Because Shakespeare is satirizing the conventional love of the pastoral romance, he has turned the usual situation around and, at the same time, exaggerated it. Instead of the lady commanding her lover to stop loving her, the lover (Ganymede) commands the lady to stop loving him and, as an added touch, commands her to love another.

The conversation is interrupted by the entrance of Oliver, who has been looking for the owners of the sheep and cottage. He recognizes Ganymede (Rosalind) and Aliena (Celia), for they have been described to him by Orlando, whom he says he has met. Holding out a bloody handkerchief, he says Orlando has asked him to give it to the youth he in jest calls Rosalind. The two girls are puzzled and ask for an explanation. Oliver says he will enlighten them, although the story he is about to reveal will do him no credit. When last Orlando left you, Oliver begins, he promised to return within an hour. As he was walking through the forest thinking about his love, he saw a ragged looking man sleeping under an oak tree. About the sleeping man's neck a snake had coiled itself and was just about to strike. Seeing Orlando approach, however, it unwound itself and slipped away. But under a nearby bush there lay a lioness watching the sleeping man and waiting for him to wake up, for lion will not prey on anything that appears dead. When Orlando came nearer, he found the sleeping man was his eldest brother. Celia interrupts to say that she has often heard Orlando describe his eldest brother as a monster, completely without any family feeling. Oliver says Orlando was quite right, for he knows very well how that eldest brother behaved. Rosalind urges him to complete the story; she wants to know whether Orlando left his brother there to be killed by the lioness. Twice he turned his back and wanted to do just that, Oliver goes on, but brotherly feeling conquered hate and Orlando attacked the beast, killed it, and with the noise, "From miserable slumber I awaked," Oliver concludes. Are you then that villain who so often tried to kill Orlando, the girls want to know. I was that villain, but I am no longer the same man, answers Oliver, for since then I have converted to a new kind of life. Here Rosalind interrupts him; she wants to know about the bloody handkerchief, and so Oliver continues with his story. After we had been reconciled to each other, he says, Orlando took me to Duke Senior, who treated me very kindly. After that Orlando led me to the cave where he lived, and when he took off his clothes we found that the lioness had torn some flesh from his arm, from which he had been bleeding all the time. Now, after the excitement and with the loss of blood, Orlando fainted, calling the name "Rosalind" as he fell. I quickly got him to come to and dressed his wound. When he was feeling a little better, he sent me here to you to excuse his absence and to give this handkerchief to the youth he in fun calls Rosalind.

On hearing the story and seeing Orlando's blood, Rosalind promptly faints. Celia has the presence of mind to call her by her assumed name: "Why, how now, Ganymede! Sweet Ganymede!" Oliver, who of course is taken in by Rosalind's male attire and knows nothing about her relationship to Orlando, says, "Many will swoon when they do look on blood." When Rosalind comes to, he jokes with her about what happened: "Be of good cheer, youth. You a man! You lack a man's heart!" (which of course is a nice piece of dramatic **irony**). Yes, Rosalind agrees that she certainly does. She now tries to make it appear that she had only pretended to swoon, and she asks Oliver to tell Orlando that her fainting had only been a joke, but Oliver is skeptical. Finally, after Rosalind insists, he says, all right, you pretended to faint; now pretend to be a man. Why, so I do, says Rosalind.

Comment

Oliver's instant conversion, never adequately motivated or explained, is typical of the conversion of villains in the final scenes of Shakespearean romantic comedy. As mentioned before, Oliver has all the equipment to make him a villain in a tragedy, but this is a comedy and thus must end happily, so we cannot be left with the uncomfortable thought that there are villains in the world. Besides, Oliver is needed as a partner for Celia, another rule of romantic comedy being that everyone must get married at the end.

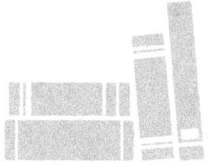

AS YOU LIKE IT

TEXTUAL ANALYSIS

ACT 5

ACT 5: SCENE 1

Touchstone and Audrey enter, engaged in conversation. Audrey has evidently been asking Touchstone when he is going to marry her, for Touchstone tells her to have patience; he is just waiting for a suitable time. Audrey (evidently not too convinced) says she cannot understand why they were not married by Sir Oliver Martext; there was nothing wrong with him, she thinks. Touchstone does not agree and then changes the subject by telling Audrey he has heard that a young native of the forest wants to marry her. Audrey says she knows the man he means and maintains that this young man is not really interested in her.

Comment

Audrey may not understand very much but she evidently is observant enough and has enough common sense to realize that bringing Touchstone to the altar might be no easy task, and that she had better marry him quickly before he changes his mind. Unfortunately for her, though, she does not realize the particular nature of his plan: to get what he wants, Touchstone has no objection to marrying Audrey; he merely objects to staying married to her.

Just then the youth in question enters. He is called William. Touchstone engages him in conversation, beginning by asking his name, age, and place of birth. Evidently impressed by Touchstone, the young man has respectfully taken off his hat, but Touchstone graciously tells him that he may keep it on. Touchstone proceeds with the interrogation of his rival. When William is asked whether he is rich, he says, "soso," which causes Touchstone to compliment him (ironically): "'soso' is good, very good, very excellent good. And yet is not, it is but soso."

Comment

William's function in the play is the same as Corin's and Auprey's: he illustrates the stupidity of real country people, particularly their inability to understand any but the simplest language. He is thus meant as a contrast to the idealized country figures of Silvius and Phebe, who are both highly articulate.

Then Touchstone asks William if he is wise, to which William replies yes. Touchstone again commends the answer, although it reminds him of the proverb which says that the fool thinks he is wise but the wise man knows himself to be a fool.

Comment

Touchstone's proverb not only brands William a fool (because he has just claimed to be wise), but also brands Touchstone wise, for no man so much knows himself to be a fool as he, since he is a fool by profession.

Touchstone then tells William that the heathen philosopher (he does not name him), upon eating a grape, would open his lips when he put it into his mouth, meaning thereby that grapes were made to eat and lips to open. Now Touchstone asks the youth whether he loves Audrey, and Williams says he does. Touchstone asks him whether he is learned, and William says no, he is not. All right, says Touchstone, then learn this of me: "To have is to have; for it is a figure [of speech] in rhetoric that drink, being poured out of a cup into a glass, by filling the one doth empty the other, for all your writers do consent that ipse [Latin for "he himself"] is he. Now you are not ipse, for I am he.

Comment

Touchstone's technique with William is the same one he previously used with Corin; he overwhelms William with nonsense which the young man is too dimwitted to perceive as nonsense. For instance, Touchstone's illustration about the heathen philosopher and the grape is sheer gibberish: Touchstone does not name the man for the very good reason that no such man existed - Touchstone has just invented him. The same applies to Touchstone's statement about rhetoric: there is no such figure of speech as Touchstone pretends to illustrate, and the "illustration" has nothing at all to do with figures of speech; it does not illustrate anything and the whole statement is nonsense, as is the following one about ipse.

When the puzzled William asks which "he" Touchstone is talking about, the latter answers, "He, sir, that must marry this woman. Therefore, you clown, abandon - which is in the vulgar [common or simple language] leave, - the society - which in the boorish [common language] is company - of this female - which in the common [language] is woman." Touchstone promises William, in the most ferocious language, that he will murder him if he does not leave Audrey alone. William takes Touchstone's advice and leaves.

Comment

Note how Touchstone emphasizes William's comical inability to understand any but the simplest language by constantly substituting simpler words for less common ones.

ACT 5: SCENE 2

In another part of the forest Orlando and Oliver are discussing the fact that Oliver has fallen in love with Celia. Orlando is astonished at the suddenness of the romance. He asks his brother how it is possible that on so short an acquaintance he could have fallen in love with Celia and Celia with him. Oliver says he cannot explain it; that that was just the way it happened. He asks Orlando to consent to their marriage, declaring that he intends to settle his father's house and money on his youngest brother and remain in the forest with his love to "live and die a shepherd." Orlando consents to Oliver's marriage and thinks the wedding should take place the next day. He will invite the Duke and his followers to the ceremony.

Comment

Oliver's lightning-swift love for Celia (still disguised as Aliena) must be numbered among the play's numerous parodies of idealized romantic love. As soon as Celia and he cast their eyes on each other, they fall in love and decide then and there to be married. Shakespeare is all in favor of love at first sight, but it should be noted that his favorite couple of the play, Orlando and Rosalind, at least talked to each other a little before preparing to take marriage vows - indeed, one of the chief uses Rosalind makes of her disguise is to find out whether Orlando really loves her, or whether he merely says he is in love with her because he finds the emotion of love a pleasant sensation. (Note, for instance, that Romeo claimed to be in love before he ever met Juliet. He is just as passionate about Rosaline as Silvius is about Phebe, yet the moment Romeo sees Juliet, Rosaline is completely forgotten. And in *Twelfth Night*, written about the same time as *As You Like It*, Duke Orsino claims to be very much in love with Olivia, while it becomes quite clear in the play that he is not in love with her at all; he is merely in love with the sensation of being in love.) The Oliver-Celia relationship is as much an exaggeration of love as the relationship between Silvius and Phebe. The love of both these couples is too idealized. The Touchstone-Audrey relationship, on the other hand, is too physical, while the Phebe-Ganymede relationship is, of course, based on a mistake. Is there then an ideal couple in the play? There is, and it is Orlando and Rosalind - but only when Rosalind's combination of romanticism and common sense prevails over Orlando. Without Rosalind to keep him in check, Orlando tends to be like Silvius, lovesick. And so by two strokes of Shakespeare's pen, Oliver turns from villain to lover.

Rosalind joins the two brothers, and Orlando repeats to her his wonder at the suddenness of Oliver's falling in love. Yes, says Rosalind, I know all about it, and indeed it was very sudden.

"For your brother and my sister no sooner met but they looked, no sooner looked but they loved, no sooner loved but they sighed, no sooner sighed by they asked one another the reason, no sooner knew the reason but they sought the remedy." And, concludes Rosalind, they are determined to be married.

Comment

That Shakespeare meant to emphasize the improbability of the Oliver-Celia match is indicated by the fact that he has both Orlando and Rosalind comment on it at length.

They will be married tomorrow, Orlando tells her, and adds that while he does not begrudge his brother the happiness, it is a painful thing to have happiness only at second hand, not to have any on your own account. Why, asks Rosalind, will I not be able to take the place of Rosalind tomorrow, as I have done until now? No, answers Orlando, I can no longer be satisfied with make - believe. Thereupon Rosalind tells him that since she sees he is a man of some intelligence, she is going to let him in on a secret. She tells Orlando that she was brought up by an expert magician and from this magician, she says, she learned to do strange things. She now promises Orlando that if he loves Rosalind as much as he claims to, he will marry her tomorrow when Oliver and Aliena are married too. Rosalind continues by saying that she knows all about Rosalind and the difficulties she has passed through, and that, if Orlando wishes, she can set her before his eyes tomorrow, in human form, and without any danger to any of the parties involved. Orlando asks Rosalind if she is speaking in earnest. Rosalind assures him that she is very much in earnest and tells Orlando to put on his best clothes tomorrow and invite all of his friends, for if he really wants to marry Rosalind, there is nothing to prevent the wedding from taking place the next day.

Comment

Orlando is no more surprised at Rosalind's statement that she can practice magic than he has been at the other strange events which have been happening in the forest, such as lions, snakes, and sheep all living together. After all, Arden is a bit like an enchanted forest - note that even villains such as Oliver and, later, Frederick, upon coming to the forest, are immediately cured of their villainy. (Arden is similar to the forest outside Athens in *A Midsummer Night's Dream*, a forest in which the king and queen of the fairies fight, Bottom's head is transformed into an ass's head, and the spirit Puck squeezes magic love potions into lovers' eyes.) The Elizabethans were very much interested in magic, ghosts, and witches, as is evidenced by the frequency with which these forms of the supernatural occur in Elizabethan drama, including Shakespeare's. (Christopher Marlowe's *Dr. Faustus* is filled with magic, as is Shakespeare's *Tempest;* witches appear in *Macbeth,* and ghosts in *Julius Caesar, Hamlet,* and *Macbeth.*) This does not mean that everyone at the close of the sixteenth century believed in magic and in spirits, but a sufficient number did; everyone was interested enough in the subject to make it a popular feature of a great many plays. King James was very much interested in witchcraft (which is probably the main reason Shakespeare put witches into *Macbeth,* written during the reign of James) and wrote a book in which he attempted to prove that witches really did exist. During the seventeenth century, skepticism about the existence of witches and other evil spirits was regarded as a sign of atheism. It was claimed that evil spirits were agents of the devil; if you did not believe in the devil's agents you did not believe in the existence of the devil; therefore you did not believe in the existence of God, for God says in the Bible that the devil exists.

Just then Silvius and Phebe enter. Phebe complains to Rosalind that she has not acted as a true gentleman should, in showing others the contents of the love letter. Rosalind replies that she has no intention of treating Phebe politely, since she does not deserve such treatment. Rosalind reminds Phebe of how much Silvius loves her and orders her not to look at anyone else, but to return his love. Phebe (thinking Rosalind is hardhearted and does not know what love means) turns to Silvius (the play's expert on romantic love) and asks him to tell "this youth" Ganymede what it means to be in love. (The answer must be quoted in full to be appreciated): "Sil. It is to be all made of sighs and tears,/ And so am I for Phebe. Phe. And I for Ganymede. Orl. And I for Rosalind. Ros. And I for no woman. Sil. It is to be able made of faith and service [to be ready to do anything one's lady asks],/ And so am I for Phebe. Phe. And I for Ganymede. Orl. And I for Rosalind. Ros. And I for no woman. Sil. It is to be all made of fantasy [imagination],/ All made of passion, and all made of wishes,/ All adoration, duty, and observance [of the wishes of one's lady],/ All humbleness, all patience and impatience,/ All purity, all trial [bearing any trial], all observance [devotion],/ And so am I for Phebe. Phe. And so am I for Ganymede. Orl. And so am I for Rosalind. Ros. And so am I for no woman." Then Phebe turns to Rosalind and asks her, if this is so, why do you blame me for loving you? Silvius turns to Phebe and asks her, if this is so, why do you blame me for loving you? Orlando, too, turns to Rosalind and asks her the same question. Startled, Rosalind asks Orlando why he asked her, "Why blame you me to love you?" Orlando explains that he had merely thought of her again as a substitute for Rosalind who, he thinks, is not really present and has not heard him.

Comment

During the "Chant of Love," Rosalind's repeated assertions that she is interested in "no woman," of course, confirm Phebe in her conviction that the youth Ganymede is hard-hearted because he has never been touched by the flames of love. It is another of the many instances of dramatic **irony** in the play. Rosalind's meaning is, of course, that she is interested only in a man, specifically, Orlando. What Silvius has to say about love is intentionally cast into the form of a formal chant (with **refrain** added by the other characters) to emphasize the formal nature (that is, the artificial nature, for the formal is always artificial) of the kind of love he is describing. This is pastoral romantic love with all its exaggeration and sentimentality. The lover is always full of sighs and tears because the lady always rejects him. She rejects him because the **convention** says she must be hard-hearted and cruel, incapable of being touched by love.

It should be noted that when Shakespeare satirizes this artificial kind of love, he is satirizing a literary **convention**, not what was actually happening in Elizabethan life. It was only in books that pastoral love was practiced. Elizabethan courtiers did not really go out into the country, dress as shepherds, and woo hard-hearted ladies dressed as shepherdesses. (But this is exactly what happened in the eighteenth century in France at the court of Marie Antoinette: lords and ladies played at being shepherds and shepherdesses according to the traditions of pastoral romance.) What Shakespeare is poking fun at is the pastoral life praised in Elizabethan literature, not the life Elizabethans actually led. He evidently does not believe that the country is necessarily better than the city or the court, or that country people, just because of their rural location, are necessarily purer and kinder than those living in the city. He does not seem to believe that courtship should be conducted according to a set pattern of rules as it is in pastoral romance. He evidently feels that the pastoral ideals set before Elizabethan readers are ridiculous and artificial.

By this time Rosalind has had quite enough of chanting **refrains** about love, which she thinks sound like "the howling of Irish wolves against the moon." She turns to Silvius and tells him that she will help him if she can. She tells Phebe that she would love her if she could and that she will marry her if she ever marries any woman, adding that she intends to be married tomorrow. Lastly, she turns again to Silvius, and promises him that he will be married tomorrow too. She charges all of them to meet her on the next day. They all promise, but the lovesick Silvius is not sure he will live so long: "I'll not fail, if I live, "he says.

Comment

As You Like It is not an attack on romantic love; it is an attack on those who are artificial and overly sentimental when in love. That is why for a while Rosalind is drawn into the artificial chant of love but checks herself when she sees how foolish they all have been. Her love for Orlando is romantic love (not, like Touchstone's for Audrey, completely sexual), but Rosalind never allows herself to become artificial and she is never sentimental for any length of time.

ACT 5: SCENE 3

Touchstone tells Audrey that the next day will be the joyful occasion of their wedding.

> Comment

The main purpose of this scene is to prepare us for the fact that Touchstone, along with Oliver and Orlando, is looking forward to being married the next day.

Audrey is looking forward to the event very much, and she hopes that eager anticipation of the marriage will not be regarded in her as any lack of respect for chastity.

> Comment

Audrey's concern about her reputation is meant to be humorous; it might have been appropriate at Court where, according to the speech of Duke Senior in Act 2, Scene 1, there were always envious people ready to do anyone a bad turn if they thought they might derive some advantage from it, but it is very much out of place here, considering her lack of social position and the Forest of Arden setting. Even if she were beautiful, there is no one in the forest with the inclination to spend time in gossip; all the other characters are wrapped up in their own affairs, either wooing or being wooed, or telling each other how much better Arden is than the Court, or being melancholy. But Audrey is supremely ugly, if we are to believe Touchstone. It is difficult to imagine how features such as hers would stir up enough envy in any Arden female to gossip about her. It is quite possible that Touchstone has been trying to teach his wife court manners, and that her concern for her reputation stems from a desire to appear more polished to her intended husband.

Two pages enter, and Touchstone asks them to sing a song for him. They oblige with the famous "It was a lover and his lass," a song praising the beauty of young love and the beauty of Spring in the country. Its **theme** is the one made famous by the Cavalier poets of the next century - that life is short and that love should be enjoyed in youth.

Comment

This scene also provides the play with another song, always welcome to the Elizabethan audience. The two previous songs praised pastoral life, while this song praises love. Pastoralism and love are what *As You Like It* is all about. Note that Shakespeare's songs do not just make music; they usually say something about the play in which they appear.

Touchstone comments (in his usual contradictory fashion) that although the song was not very profound, yet it was sung very badly. One of the pages defends the singing, claiming they did not lose the time - that is, they kept the proper beat of the music. Touchstone cannot resist a pun on "time," saying, "By my troth yes. I count it but time lost to hear such a foolish song. God buy you [God be with you], and God mend [improve] your voices!"

Comment

It is possible that Touchstone is here parodying the actions of Jaques in Act 2, Scene 5, in which Jaques begs Amiens to sing and then criticizes what has been sung. Note that Touchstone does exactly the same thing here, and that this kind of behavior is not usual for him.

ACT 5: SCENE 4

It is the next day, and Duke Senior, Amiens, Jaques, Orlando, Oliver, and Celia have gathered to watch Rosalind perform her promised magic. The Duke asks Orlando whether he believes Rosalind can do all she says she can. Orlando answers that sometimes he believes her and sometimes he does not, depending on how optimistic he is feeling at the time. Rosalind, Silvius, and Phebe enter. Rosalind once more reminds the group of their various agreements. She wants to know if the Duke will keep his promise to bestow his daughter Rosalind on Orlando, should she, Ganymede, be able to make Rosalind appear in the forest. The Duke says he would do so even if he had to give kingdoms with her as her dowry. Rosalind asks Orlando if he will marry Rosalind when she appears, to which Orlando answers that he would do so were the king of all the kingdoms of the earth. Now speaking about her assumed personality of the young man Ganymede, Rosalind asks Phebe if she is willing to marry her. Phebe answers she would do so even if she were to die for it one hour later. But, says Rosalind, if for any reason you refuse to marry me, you agree to marry Silvius. Yes, that is the bargain, replies Phebe. Lastly, Rosalind asks Silvius whether he will marry Phebe if she consents, to which Silvius answers that he would do so even if it meant death. All right, says Rosalind, I have promised to make everyone happy; I have to leave for a short time to attend to these matters. She once again charges each member of the group to keep his promise, as she will keep hers.

After Celia and Rosalind leave, the Duke tells Orlando that there is something about Ganymede which reminds him of his daughter Rosalind. Orlando, too, says he has been struck by the resemblance; he says the first time he saw Ganymede he thought he was Rosalind's brother. However, he explains to the Duke, he has learned that Ganymede was born in Arden and tutored in the study of magic by his magician uncle, and so he knows the young man could not be the Duke's relative.

Comment

Note that both Silvius and Phebe, the sentimental pastoral figures of the play, say that they will die if necessary, so long as they can have their respective sweethearts, Silvius longing for Phebe and Phebe longing for Ganymede. Their attitude toward love recalls the words of Rosalind in Act 4, Scene 1: "Men have died from time to time and worms have eaten them, but not for love."

Touchstone and Audrey join the others. This is too much for Jaques, who professes to think that there must be another flood approaching and that all the couples who have gathered to be married have really come to take shelter in Noah's Ark like the animals, two by two. Seeing Touchstone and Audrey (and continuing his comparison of the animals coming to the Ark), Jaques says, "Here comes a pair of very strange beasts, which in all tongues are called fools."

Comment

In his commentary on the couples assembling to be married, Jaques demonstrates his usual critical attitude. He calls Touchstone and Audrey fools, because he thinks they are not suited to each other, as he has previously told Touchstone. Note, incidentally, that while both Touchstone and Jaques usually make critical comments on what is happening, Jaques' comments tend to be more biting than Touchstone's, and not nearly so witty.

Touchstone greets the company, whereupon Jaques introduces him to the Duke. This is the fool I met in the forest, says Jaques, and he swears he has been a courtier. Why, says Touchstone, let any man who doubts the truth of that claim put me to the test. I have taken part in formal dancing. I have flattered a lady. I have been crafty with my friend, deceptively friendly with my enemy. I have bankrupt three tailors by not paying their bills for the many clothes they have made me. I have had four quarrels and was almost involved in a duel because of one of them. Jaques asks what the outcome was. Touchstone replies that he and his opponent met "and found the quarrel was upon the seventh cause." (Touchstone explains the meaning of this statement a few lines later.)

Comment

Touchstone's picture of the typical courtier is, of course, a satirical one. What is interesting about it is that it contains elements of the stock pastoral view of city and, especially, court life. Note the emphasis on deceit and flattery, which Duke Senior specifically singles out in Act 2, Scene 1, as qualities present at court but absent from pastoral life. It seems that in *As You Like It*, Shakespeare not only satirizes pastoralism by bringing a court fool into the country to expose the folly of country bumpkins, but also satirizes certain aspects of the courtier by having that same fool adopt the pastoral **convention** of criticizing the court.

Elizabethan men of fashion were very much interested in clothes, on which they sometimes spent enormous sums. Unlike the style of today, men's clothing was just as colorful, if not more so, than women's. If one wanted to be really fashionable, one bought his clothes abroad, for English taste, as explained previously, was thought to be inferior to that of other major European countries. Included in the usual **satire** of the Englishman who has traveled abroad (such as the one between Rosalind and Jaques in Act 4, Scene 1) is the point that while he despised his own country's taste in clothes, he showed poor taste in selecting his clothes from other countries. He is usually pictured as wearing a variety of objects which do not match, such as a Spanish hat, a German jacket, Italian trousers, and French shoes. In the sixteenth century the quality of the clothes one wore was supposed to distinguish one's rank. There were actually proclamations saying that no one below a certain rank could wear certain items of apparel. But since Elizabethans were constantly breaking these rules, there were many complaints from noblemen that it was impossible to tell who was titled and who was not.

Jaques is delighted by the way Touchstone is speaking, and the Duke also expresses his pleasure with him, whereupon Touchstone feels compelled to explain why he is present among those waiting to be married: "I press in here, sir, amongst the rest of the country copulatives, to swear and to forswear [to swear the marriage vows and to be forsworn because he has no intention of keeping them - that is, of remaining married to Audrey], according as marriage binds and blood breaks. A poor virgin sir, an ill-favored [ugly] thing, sir, but mine own." He goes on to explain that he is marrying Audrey just because she is ugly and so will have no opportunity to be unfaithful to him.

Comment

Touchstone's completely unromantic, sexual idea of marriage (meant to contrast especially with that of Silvius) is emphasized by the sexual puns he makes when explaining his presence in the marriage group:

1. "Country" is a pun on (a) those living in the country and (b) also relates to the female sexual organ.

2. "Copulatives" is a pun on (a) those to be joined together in marriage and (b) those about to engage in copulation, i.e., sexual intercourse.

3. "Blood breaks" is a pun referring to (a) the flowing of blood after the breaking of the hymen in the vagina after sexual intercourse, and (b) the stirring up of his blood, that is, sexual desire, which will eventually cause him to leave Audrey for another and thus "break" their marriage.

Quarrel was on the seventh cause. Touchstone explains that he and his Jaques now asks Touchstone to explain what he meant by finding the opponent found that the cause of the quarrel was a lie "seven times removed," on which expression he proceeds to elaborate. I did not like the way a certain courtier cut his beard, begins Touchstone, and I wrote to tell him so.

Comment

Elizabethans were very proud of their beards and the way they were cut, so that insults about beards were common. Note Rosalind's remark about beards in the epilogue of this play. In *A Midsummer Night's Dream*, Act 1, Scene 2, Bottom, thinking about acting a part on the stage, is mainly concerned with what kind of beard he should wear for the part.

Touchstone continues: He sent me word that if I did not think his beard was cut well, he thought it was; this is called the "Retort Courteous." If I wrote him again that I thought it was not well cut, he would write me that he cut his beard to please himself; this is called the "Quip [sarcastic jest] Modest." If again I said his beard was not well cut, he would say I was unfit to give an opinion on the subject; this is called the "Reply Churlish" [surly, boorish]. If again I said it was not well cut, he would answer that I did not speak the truth; this is called the "Reproof Valiant." If I again said it was not well cut; he would say that I was lying; this is called the "Countercheck Quarrelsome." From here the quarrel would proceed to the "Lie Circumstantial" [an indirect accusation that your opponent is a liar], and finally to the "Lie Direct" [a direct accusation that your opponent is a liar, regarded as a deadly insult, and requiring a duel to redeem the honor of the insulted party]. Well, asks Jaques, and how often did you say that the courtier's beard was not well cut? I did not dare go any further than the "Lie Circumstantial," answers Touchstone, and he did not dare to go as far as the "Lie Direct," so we never did fight a duel.

Jaques is impressed and asks Touchstone if he can once again go over the various degrees of the lie he has just explained. Of course, says Touchstone; I know them by heart, for there are books written on how to quarrel properly, just as there are books to teach good manners. He runs over the stages once again, and then explains that all of the degrees of accusation may be safely indulged in without danger of fighting a duel, except the last one, the "Lie Direct." But even here you may escape safely, adds Touchstone, if you are careful to qualify what you say with an "if." He says he can recall the case of a quarrel which seven judges could not patch up, but when the two opponents actually met face to face, one of them thought of an "if," such as, "If you said so, then I said so," and so they shook hands and swore eternal friendship.

Comment

The entire passage is a **satire** on quarreling. Note that what Shakespeare is making fun of is not the fact that people quarrel, but that it was customary among Elizabethan gentlemen to quarrel according to certain rules. Thus Shakespeare's ridicule of a formula for quarreling - on which, as Touchstone tells us, there were even "how to" books written - should be associated with the main **theme** of this play: Shakespeare's **satire** on the **convention** of pastoral love. Both conventions led people to substitute artificial behavior for natural emotions. Shakespeare seems to feel that it is ridiculous to get angry according to a rule book, just as it is ridiculous to fall in love according to the requirements of a rule book. In practice, the Elizabethan gentleman's attitude toward quarreling had far more serious consequences than his attitude toward love. Almost anything was regarded as grounds for a quarrel - for instance, refusing to yield one's place closest to the walls of the houses as one was walking along the street. We can see an instance of just such a quarrel in *Romeo and Juliet,* Act 1, Scene 1, when Sampson says, "I will take the wall (go closest to the wall) of any man or maid of Montague's." (Remember that no matter where Shakespeare's plays are supposed to be taking place or what the names of his characters, Shakespeare is actually thinking of conditions in England and of Englishmen.) This was an age without a police force as we know it, an age in which all men carried weapons of some sort (noblemen carried rapiers, commoners, swords), an age, consequently, in which quarrels very often ended not only in bloodshed but even in death. In such an atmosphere of violence (not dissimilar to the American Wild West), books which taught men to look for insults and how to deal with them were not only ridiculous but also dangerous.

A good example of how dangerous such an artificial concept of personal honor could be is provided in *Hamlet*. (Remember that while *Hamlet* is set in medieval Denmark, Shakespeare is really thinking of early seventeenth-century London.) In Act 5, Scene 2, Laertes tells Hamlet that although he would personally like to accept Hamlet's apology, he cannot, at the moment, since their quarrel concerns his personal honor. He must first consult experts in the matter, and only if they tell him that he can be reconciled with Hamlet without loss of prestige, will he accept the offered apology. Shakespeare emphasizes the artificiality of such a concept of honor by having Laertes make this speech just before he kills Hamlet in the most dishonorable fashion imaginable: a crooked fencing match.

Turning to the Duke, Jaques asks him whether he does not think Touchstone is a wonderful fellow. "He's as good at anything and yet a fool," he points out. To this the Duke replies that Touchstone "uses his folly like a stalking-horse [a horse the hunter would hide behind when stalking game, so that he would not be seen or smelled], and under the presentation [under the cover] of that he shoots his wit."

Comment

Jaques' remark about Touchstone once again reminds us of the function of the licensed fool in Shakespeare's plays. Because everything he says is, according to **convention**, supposed to be foolish, and therefore not to be resented, he is at liberty to criticize anyone he pleases, including his social superiors.

To the accompaniment of soft music, the figure of Hymen, the god of marriage, enters. With him are Rosalind and Celia.

Hymen says that there is rejoicing in heaven when the paths of earthly men run smoothly and all their difficulties are removed.

Comment

The introduction of the god Hymen once again demonstrates the unrealistic nature of the play. It is thought that perhaps the entire last part of the play, including the introduction of Hymen and the dances performed to celebrate the marriage ceremonies, was inserted after the original composition of the play on the occasion of its performance at the wedding of some nobleman.

Hymen then turns to the Duke and tells him to receive his daughter, who has been brought to the forest for the purpose of being joined to the man she loves. (In stage presentations of the play, it is customary to have Rosaliod remain heavily veiled in white up to this point, so that no one knows who she is.) Now she removes the veil from her face and reveals herself as Rosalind. She turns to the Duke and says, "To you I give myself, for I am yours." Then she addresses Orlando in the same words. The Duke says that unless his sight is deceiving him, this must be Rosalind, and Orlando echoes what the Duke says. Phebe takes one look at the transformed Ganymede with whom she had been in love and says, "If sight and shape be true,/ Why then, my love adieu!" Hymen now takes charge of the proceedings and addresses the four couples before him. To Orlando and Rosalind he says that no troubles will ever part them. To Oliver and Celia he says that their love will last as long as they live. To Phebe he says that either she must marry Silvius or be married to a woman (Rosalind). To Touchstone and Audrey he says (in a comment on the lack of warmth of Touchstone's love for his wife and on Audrey's looks), "You and you are sure together./ As the winter to foul weather." All join in singing a hymn in praise of marriage, after which the Duke joyfully embraces his daughter and his niece. Phebe suddenly sees Silvius in a new light; she says she will marry him not only because she promised she would do so, but because she finds she has fallen in love with him!

Comment

Phebe's sudden love for Silvius, whom she has scornfully rejected for so long, is merely another of the numerous improbable incidents in the play, comparable to the sudden conversion of Oliver and his equally sudden love for Celia. The purpose of Phebe's change of mind is, of course, to ensure that by the play's end all the lovers will be paired off and everything will end happily.

All of a sudden the celebrants are interrupted by the appearance of a new character. He is Jaques De Boys, the second son of Sir Rowland, and brother to Oliver and Orlando. (He was briefly mentioned by Orlando in his speech which opened the play.) Jaques tells the company who he is and announces that he has important news for them. He says that Duke Frederick, having heard that many important men were daily leaving his court and joining his exiled brother in Arden, prepared a mighty army. He led them into the forest with the purpose of capturing and killing his brother, thus removing a source of possible rebellion against his rule. But, reports Jaques De Boys, when Frederick came to the outskirts of Arden he met an old hermit. This hermit prevailed on him not only to abandon his plan of killing his brother, but also to abandon the world and become a hermit, too.

> **Comment**

The sudden conversion of Frederick is probably (excepting the introduction of the god Hymen) the least credible event of the play. Once again it must be remembered that in this comedy Shakespeare is not interested in creating psychologically accurate minor characters. The whole function of Frederick is to provide the play with a banished Duke to praise the pastoral life of Arden. Now that this particular function has been fulfilled, he must no longer be allowed to stand in the way of the play's happy ending. To have him die or be killed would introduce too solemn a note at a time when gaiety is called for. His conversion, therefore, allows the play to close in an atmosphere of general harmony. Through that conversion, all the wrongs existing at the beginning of the play have been righted by its end.

As a result, Frederick has restored to Duke Senior and his followers everything which was taken from them, and they are free to return from exile at any time they wish. Duke Senior welcomes the news on behalf of himself and his company. First, he says, they will proceed with the wedding rites, and then all who have endured bitter exile with him will return to their lands and their former dignity.

> **Comment**

The Duke's comment that his exile has been bitter demonstrates once again that his praise of pastoral life was mere rationalization. Note that he and his courtiers rush back to the Court they profess to despise the moment they are given the opportunity.

But Jaques, when he hears that Frederick has decided to become a hermit and abandon the glitter of the court, resolves to stay with him in Arden.

Comment

Jaques' resolve to remain with the pastoral life, now that he no longer has to, shows that his criticism of that life was as much a pose for him as was the Duke's praise of pastoralism. Jaques is in favor of neither court nor country; he is in favor only of being against everything everybody else is for.

Jaques bids farewell to Duke Senior and wishes him good fortune in his restored honor. Likewise, he gives his best wishes to Orlando, Oliver, and Silvius, parting from the latter, with, "You to a long and well-deserved bed." Lastly he turns to Touchstone and Audrey; he leaves them to their quarreling and expresses the opinion that their marriage will last about two months. The scene ends with a dance in celebration of the multiple weddings.

Comment

It is ironic that in his parting remark to Silvius, Jaques should stress the sexual aspect of that young man's union with Phebe. Of all the concepts of love expressed by the various characters in the play, that of Silvius is most idealized - and therefore furthest removed from the physical. Once again, through Jaques, Shakespeare reminds us that love is neither all romantic passion, as Silvius thinks, nor all sex, as Touchstone thinks, but a little of both, as Rosalind realizes.

AS YOU LIKE IT

When the play is over, Rosalind appears on the stage to deliver an epilogue (a speech by an actor at the end of the play requesting the applause of the audience). Rosalind says that while it is not the custom to have the epilogue delivered by the leading lady, there is nothing wrong with it. She admits that just as a good wine needs no advertisement to make people appreciate it, so a good play should need no epilogue. Yet, she says, people who sell good hines do not hesitate to tell customers how good the wines are, and good plays are improved by good epilogues.

Comment

What Rosalind actually says is that "good wine needs no bush." The bush was the sign of the wine seller, and it hung outside his shop. In an age when quite a number of people could not read, picture signs were used to tell customers what a particular shop contained: A relic of this custom today is the barber's pole.

You can see what a position I am in then, Rosalind continues to the audience, without a good epilogue to deliver to you at the end of a good play.

Comment

Notice Shakespeare's modesty here, which was not a very common Renaissance virtue. This quality was so noticeable in Shakespeare that he was especially praised for it by his contemporaries.

Now, Rosalind says, since I have no intention of getting down on my knees and begging you to be pleased with this play, there is only one thing I can do: I shall win you over by the use of magic. And so I charge you, ladies, to like as much of this play as pleased you. I charge you, gentlemen, for the love you have for the ladies, to like it for their sake.

Comment

Since Rosalind had pretended to be a magician in the play, it is appropriate for her to declare that she intends to practice magic on the audience.

Now if I were really a woman (the actor, of course, was a boy), Rosalind concludes, I would kiss as many of you men as wore beards which pleased me, had faces I liked, and breath that did not stink. And I am sure that as many as have good beards, faces, and breaths "will, for my kind offer, when I make curtsy, bid me farewell" (by applauding).

Comment

Elizabethans did not have modern notions of personal cleanliness. Ladies especially thought that too much washing ruined the skin, and taking care of the teeth was unheard of. As a result, Elizabethans smelled quite strong generally and tried to cover up with perfume instead of soap. Unlike most of his contemporaries, Shakespeare seems to have been very sensitive to bad smells.

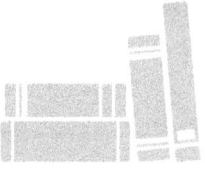

AS YOU LIKE IT

CHARACTER ANALYSES

Rosalind

Rosalind is without question the most attractive character of the play, as well as the most important, from the point of view of the plot. What makes Rosalind so attractive is not only the energy and brains she displays disguised as Ganymede, but, more important, her ability to laugh at herself and her predicament. When Rosalind pokes fun at Orlando's sentimental tendencies, as he swears he is about to die for love, she is poking fun at the same tendencies in herself. With very little encouragement she could be as sentimental as Orlando, or even Silvius, but she knows herself and so keeps herself in check. She is our favorite because she is just as much in love as Silvius and would like to act as lovesick as he, but she pulls herself together and instead acts like the man she is pretending to be.

We get a taste of Rosalind's ingenuity in love, which later makes her hit on the happy idea of having Orlando woo her while she is disguised, at the moment she first falls in love. To have another opportunity to talk to the young wrestler, she pretends to Celia that she has heard him call them back. We have a demonstration of her courage in her spirited reply to Duke Frederick's accusation that she is a traitor. Her initiative is again displayed in her suggestion to disguise herself as a man to make their journey safer, and to take along Touchstone to provide entertainment. It is also Rosalind who, though just reminded of her seemingly hopeless love for Orlando by Silvius' plea to Phebe, arranges to buy the house and sheep in Arden, so they will be able to sustain themselves. How deeply she is in love is demonstrated later when, although desperate to hear Celia's account of meeting Orlando, she keeps interrupting Celia with comments on each detail. Her skill is again in evidence when she turns her opening conversation with Orlando to the subject of love, and proposes her scheme of mock wooing. (Note that Shakespeare alternates between incidents which show Rosalind's love for Orlando and her adeptness in doing something about it. During the mock courtship, Orlando is supposed to be wooing Rosalind, but it is really Rosalind who is wooing. She has promised to cure him of his love by making Rosalind unattractive to him; what she does instead is teach him how to love Rosalind all the more.) Just before Orlando's first lesson, we again see the depth of Rosalind's love as he impatiently waits for her pupil to arrive. She is assailed by doubts about his sincerity, but she will not let anyone else speak against him. Again, after the lesson, she reveals her love to us - and almost gives the show away when Orlando tells her that he must leave her for two hours: "Alas, dear love, I cannot lack thee two hours!"

The classic incident which demonstrates at the same time Rosalind's love and her ability to keep her sanity even though in love is the occasion when Oliver shows her Orlando's bloodstained handkerchief. Rosalind is so overcome that she faints, but she is cool enough to pretend to have pretended to faint, thus preserving her disguise. Rosalind is obviously Shakespeare's ideal lover. She is neither sentimental about love like Silvious, nor cynical about love like Touchstone, but just right.

Orlando

An analysis of Orlando yields the somewhat surprising conclusion that he is rather dull. One wonders what such a spirited and clever girl as Rosalind sees in him; hopefully, when he is married, he will learn something from his wife. That she teaches him throughout the play is evident, but the subject he learns in her class is not the one for which he is registered. As mentioned before, Rosalind has no intention of curing her lover of love. What she does is rid him of the Silvius side of his nature. When Orlando first comes into Arden, he decorates the trees with moonish poems written in bad verse, but Rosalind scoffs at his conviction that a single frown from her would kill him.

What first strikes us about Orlando, however, is his courage and strength. He stands up to his older brother and is not afraid to face a professional wrestler against heavy odds. He displays the same courage and physical strength toward the end of the play when he saves his brother from a hungry lioness. We get insight into his basic goodness from his regard for the old man, Adam, and from the latter's obvious affection for Orlando. His loyalty and courage are again displayed when he is ready to do single-handed battle with Duke Senior's entire retinue to provide Adam with food. He approaches cleverness only when he bests Jaques in an encounter of wits, but this, of course, is not a very difficult feat.

Celia

Celia is not a very fully developed character and is quite overshadowed by Rosalind. Her main function is to provide Rosalind with someone to whom she can confide her love for Orlando; Touchstone is hardly a person to listen sympathetically to Rosalind's descriptions of her love. By having Rosalind continually tell Celia how she feels about Orlando, Shakespeare avoids having Rosalind declare her passion in numerous asides or soliloquies.

Celia's most outstanding quality is her affection for Rosalind. It is quite possible that the attachment of the two girls is also a target of Shakespeare's **satire**. The Renaissance valued friendship even more highly than love, and pastoral romances are filled with characters whose ideal friendship survives the most improbable tests. (Shakespeare himself portrays such a friendship seriously in his earlier play *The Two Gentlemen of Verona*. His pattern was usually to accept a **convention** seriously, until he grew tired of it; then he made fun of it.) These ideal friendships were always between men; Shakespeare's depiction of such a friendship between women is a novelty in itself.

At the beginning of the play, Celia shares as much of the action and dialogue as Rosalind. In the conversations with Le Beau and Touchstone she is just as witty as her cousin. It is only when she leaves her father's court and the Rosalind-Orlando relationship begins to dominate the play, that she retires to a secondary role. In the forest, since she is not yet in love, she is often cooler and more sensible than her cousin. She even teases Rosalind about her feeling for Orlando, an ironic note, since in the end she falls in love even more suddenly than her cousin.

Touchstone

Touchstone, the licensed fool, is the real critic of the play (in contrast to Jaques, who thinks he has a monopoly on that role). It is by his sanity and practicality that the madness and sentimentality of the other characters is judged. This is not to say that Touchstone is Shakespeare's ideal character. He is as extreme in his materialism as the others are in their various affectations. Touchstone is contrast. For instance, neither Touchstone nor Silvius is the ideal lover; the ideal lies somewhere between the two extremes. Touchstone's main function is to expose pretense, and there is a lot of pretense to be exposed in Arden. In contrast to Duke Senior's extravagant praise of country life, Touchstone says that Arden is a very uncomfortable place and that he would have done much better to have stayed at home. When Rosalind gets foolishly sentimental over Orlando, after hearing Silvius' lament of unrequited love, Touchstone provides realistic ridicule to demonstrate the absurdity of Silvius and Rosalind wallowing in self-pity. His story of his behavior in love is so obviously ridiculous that we can see that the behavior of Silvius and, to some extent, of Rosalind, is only slightly less ridiculous. By **parody**, Touchstone pierces through the pretense of pastoral love. He unmasks Jaques' stupidity in the same fashion. On their first meeting, Touchstone takes his measure and demonstrates what a fool Jaques is by repeating to him just the sort of shallow nonsense Jaques passes off to others as profound thought.

Touchstone's meeting with Corin does not expose any pretense in the old shepherd, for he has none. The pretense which is exposed by the meeting is that real shepherds talk like Silvius. They are not capable of sophisticated thought and conversation, as they are in stock pastoral romances. It is to demonstrate the absurdity of this pastoral **convention** that Corin's simple-mindedness is emphasized, as well as his inability to understand precisely that courtly language in which the conventional shepherd of pastoral romance spoke.

Touchstone's conversations with William and Audrey serve the same function; they show the audience that real country people are not always as clever and articulate as they are represented in pastoral romances. Touchstone's wooing of Audrey, with its emphasis on the sexual, is meant to contrast with the overly idealistic wooing of Phebe by Silvius, who does not seem to be aware of sex at all. For him Phebe might as well be some heavenly creature without a body.

Jaques

Jaques (pronounced "jake-ways") is the self-appointed critic of the play. Shakespeare occasionally uses him to criticize Arden and its inhabitants, but more often his function is to demonstrate that critics themselves are open to criticism. When in a lengthy speech, he criticizes the Duke for killing deer, it soon becomes evident that Jaques is much more interested in how many comparisons he can make between the fate of animals and men, than in the fate of any deer the Duke may have shot. When Amiens sings a song in praise of the pastoral life, Jaques sings about its silliness. This is one of the few instances in which Jaques makes a point Shakespeare seems to want to make himself. But Jaques is not sincere in his criticism of the country. Ironically, he is the only one who really likes Arden, for he chooses to remain there when all the others leave. And so makes fun of Amiens' song not out of conviction but merely because he cannot stop criticizing. He is a hypocrite, and his hypocrisy is further emphasized by Duke Senior. When Jaques envies Touchstone in his position of licensed fool, because as such Touchstone can make fun of others without fear of retaliation, the Duke reminds Jaques (and in this way informs the audience) of the fact that Jaques himself has been guilty of all the sins and follies he wants to criticize in other people. Jacques' answer that he will not do any harm to the innocent because only the guilty will be hurt by what he says was the stock answer of Elizabethan satirists to criticism of their activity. Jaques embodies Shakespeare's opinion of the satirists who were flourishing just when he wrote *As You Like It*.

Jaques' comment on life in general, contained in his "Seven Ages" speech, is a bitter one. However, we learn nothing about him which might make us believe such bitterness to be warranted on his part - neither Rosalind nor Orlando, who would have had good reason, are bitter about life - and everything that happens in the play contradicts what he says; everybody but him lives happily ever afterwards. We must conclude, therefore, the "Seven Ages" speech does not represent Jaques' true feeling about life. He thinks it fashionable to be a discontented critic, but manages to fool no one with his pose but himself. Rosalind tells him that his affection of continual melancholy is stupid, and Orlando gets him to admit, by means of a pathetically simple device, that he is a fool.

Silvius

Silvius is the conventional shepherd of the pastoral romance. His hopeless love for Phebe is rejected with cold scorn. He is the typical pastoral hero, much more articulate and polished than a real shepherd would be, and he knows almost nothing about keeping sheep. Because of his great love, he can neither sleep nor eat, and should Phebe order him to kill himself, he would be quite prepared to do so. He is convinced he is slowly dying from Phebe's frowns. In Silvius, Shakespeare concentrates all that is absurd about pastoralism.

Note that in satirizing Silvius, Shakespeare is not poking fun at Elizabethan life but at Elizabethan literature. No such figures really roamed the streets of Shakespeare's London, and certainly no such shepherds kept Elizabethan sheep. But shepherds such as Silvius and Phebe were what Elizabethans loved to read about in their "escape" literature, and Shakespeare is suggesting that, even as escape, the pastoral ideal is absurd.

Phebe

Just as Silvius is the conventional lover, so is Phebe the conventional lady of pastoral romance. Their names are derived from the work of the Greek poet Theocritus, who wrote in the third century B.C.; by the time *As You Like It* was written, many pastoral figures had borne these names.

Phebe rejects the advances of Silvius, not because she is particularly averse to him, but because the rules say she should be hard-hearted. The rapidity with which she agrees to marry Silvius when she finds out that Ganymede is a girl shows that Phebe had nothing against Silvius on his own account. The absurdity of Silvius feeling inferior to Phebe (the conventional lover always feels inferior to his lady, and has to do mighty feats to win her approval) is pointed out by Rosalind; it seems that Silvius is very handsome, but that Phebe is rather ugly.

The Phebe-Ganymede mixup further satirizes pastoral love, for Phebe, who all the while has been scorning love according to the fashion of the day, is suddenly hit by a love so powerful that she forgets all about the fashion. In fact, she turns the **convention** upside down as she starts to run after Ganymede and openly declares her love for him. The final thrust occurs when she, instead of giving orders to the man, accepts commandments from Ganymede. The ultimate absurdity is, of course, that Phebe's grand passion turns out to be misplaced - her idol Ganymede is really a woman.

Duke Senior

Duke Senior, banished from his own court by his brother Frederick, tries very hard to like Arden, but he does not quite succeed. He proclaims, for the benefit of his followers, and perhaps for his own, too, that it is much better to be in the forest where there are no false flatterers or envious plotters (like his brother). But when he hears of Orlando's tribulations, he turns to Jaques and says, "Thou seest we are not all alone unhappy," revealing his true feelings about this situation. At the end of the play he admits that he and his followers "have endured shrewd [bitter] days and nights," and he is only too happy to return to the "corrupt" court.

Oliver

Oliver is one of the two villains of the play. His first function is to motivate Orlando to go to Arden by a plot on his life. His second function is to provide Celia with a husband at the end of the play. Oliver's villainy is manifested by the following:

1. his denying Orlando his just inheritance

2. his harsh treatment of the good old man Adam

3. his two plots to murder Orlando

4. his lying about Orlando

5. his own admission that he has been lying about Orlando

6. his indirect admission that he is evil, when he declares that he hates Orlando even though he knows Orlando is good.

7. the fact that even his own servants dislike him and prefer his brother.

Oliver's own admission that he is evil places him in the ranks of the great Shakespearean villains like Iago. It is only because the play is a comedy that *As You Like It* ends happily. Oliver's sudden conversion and equally sudden love for Celia parodies similar improbable happenings in Elizabethan pastoral romances.

Frederick

While Oliver is the private villain of the play, in that his crimes are against individuals and not against the state, Frederick is the typical political villain. He has usurped the throne from the lawful ruler. In rebelling against lawfully constituted authority, he has committed the most serious political sin possible. According to Elizabethan theory, to rebel against the king is to rebel against God. Thus Frederick is comparable to *Richard III, Macbeth,* and *Hamlet's* Claudius, all usurpers who murdered to obtain the throne. Near the end of *As You Like It*, Frederick is about to commit murder to keep his throne secure. Like all usurpers, Frederick is unsure of himself. He is afraid (like Macbeth) that his usurpation may have taught others the way to power. This is why he banishes Rosalind. He is afraid that she might be a rallying point for her father's supporters (just as

Queen Elizabeth was afraid that Mary Queen of Scots would be a rallying point for her enemies).

In terms of the plot, Frederick is responsible for getting Duke Senior, Jaques, Rosalind, Celia, Touchstone, Oliver, and finally himself to Arden, where the main action of the play takes place. His sudden conversion, parallel to Oliver's, removes the last obstacle to happiness, as well as parodying similar unlikely conversions of the pastoral romance.

Adam

Adam is the loyal retainer of medieval and Renaissance fiction. He is the personification of virtue. As such, he provides a backdrop against which Oliver and Orlando can show their true characters: we can see right away that Oliver is evil because he mistreats Adam, and we can see that Orlando is good because of his kindness to the old man. Adam's willingness to give Orlando his life savings is one of the many exaggerations of the play for the purpose of **parody**. (In Adam, extravagant and improbable loyalty is thus made fun of; in Silvius, the exaggeration is love; in Jaques, melancholy; and in Touchstone, realism.) Adam also is responsible for bringing Orlando into contact with the Duke in Arden, when Orlando goes to seeks food for the old man. These functions fulfilled, Adam drops out of sight in the play. (One would think that after he had given Orlando all his money, he would at least have been invited to the wedding! Seriously, it is quite likely that the actor who played Adam also took the part of either Hymen or Jaques De Boys, and therefore Adam had to disappear abruptly. Minor roles were often "doubled" in the Elizabethan theatre.)

MINOR CHARACTERS

Corin, William, and Audrey all have the same function. Their purpose is to provide realistic contrast to the artificial figures of Silvius and Phebe. They are real country yokels, while Silvius and Phebe are literary imitations. That is why their simple-mindedness and limited vocabulary is emphasized; it is meant to contrast with the polish and literary speech of the pastoral lover and his cruel lady. Audrey's presence in the play, of course, also provides Touchstone with a wife in a marriage which parodies all the others.

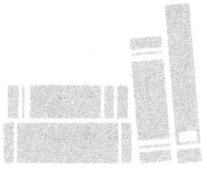

AS YOU LIKE IT

CRITICAL COMMENTARY

John Palmer (*Comic Characters of Shakespeare*) points out that Shakespeare's source for his play was sophisticated and mannered in sentiment. While Shakespeare kept most of his source's characters and incidents, he completely changed the tone. For instance, the quarrel of the brothers in Lodge is a "desperate feud," whereas in Shakespeare it is a "boyish squabble." (There is nothing very "boyish" about Oliver's intention to murder Orlando.) Lodge spends as much time on the bad brother's conversion as on the adventures of Rosalind, while Shakespeare has a lightning conversion and has Oliver marry Celia. Lodge ends his pastoral with a battle between the banished Duke and his brother in which the usurper is killed, while Shakespeare ends his play with marriage ceremonies, after Frederick's conversion.

Thomas M. Parrott (*Shakespearean Comedy*) sees *As You Like It* as a play written in haste. He thinks that the wedding celebration may have been added after its original composition, on the occasion of its performance at some nobleman's wedding. Perhaps the title of the play refers to the Elizabethan love for the pastoral of which Shakespeare gently makes fun. Commenting on the language of the play, Parrott notes that whenever sentiment prevails Shakespeare uses verse, but when the stress is on character development and **satire**, prose is the vehicle of expression. As for the play's setting, he says that while Lodge's forest (see comment on "source") was the Ardennes of France, Shakespeare's Arden, in spite of the lion, is the forest of his native Warwickshire.

H. B. Charlton (*Shakespearean Comedy*) thinks that Shakespeare's Arden is not an ideal world. People feel cold there and have to shoot deer in order to eat. It has surly landlords, as is evidenced by Corin's account of his master. And Arden is only an interlude in life - Rosalind and Orlando return to civilization to face its problems.

C. L. Barber (*Shakespeare's Festive Comedy*) compares the Forest of Arden to the wood outside Athens in *A Midsummer Night's Dream*. It is a place free from ordinary limitations, a place where the folly of love can flourish. The sense of freedom in Arden comes from a release from the tensions of Frederick's corrupt court.

According to D. L. Stevenson (*The Love-Game Comedy*), Shakespeare peoples Arden with characters who **parody** their literary originals. Orlando is the conventional pastoral Petrarchan lover, but he must first take lessons in the art of suffering from Rosalind! (This is not so. Rosalind promises to cure Orlando of love. What she does do is make him fall more deeply into love. She neither promises to teach Orlando how to suffer in love, nor does do so.) Audrey is a **parody** of a milkmaid and Phebe of the scornful shepherdess. Besides **parody** of character, the comments that characters make on each other are important. For instance, Silvius is criticized by Corin,

Touchstone, and Rosalind, who points out to Silvius that he is in love with an idea, not with the unattractive Phebe.

Bertrand Evans (*Shakespeare's Comedies*) finds that although the first two acts contain many contrasts between the good country and the evil court, the ultimate criticism of life the play makes it a gentle one. Real villainy cannot endure in the atmosphere presented.

Palmer notes that *As You Like It* is one of the types of plays mentioned by Polonius in *Hamlet* as "pastoral-comical." This type of play was coming into fashion at the beginning of the seventeenth century. The pastoral satisfies the desire of civilized people to assume simplicity. It was very much in fashion when Shakespeare wrote the first draft of his play in 1593. Palmer goes on to show that while the pastoral pretended to be simple, it was actually very learned. Shepherds court their mistresses in complicated verse forms, while shepherdesses quote Ovid and Latin proverbs. Shakespeare enthusiastically adopts the **conventions** of the pastoral at the same time as mocking them. He provides an ideal pastoral world in Arden - but he peoples that world with non-ideal characters; human nature does not change in Arden.

In the view of S.C. Sen Gupta (*Shakespearean Comedy*), there is no other comedy in which minor characters are so important as in *As You Like It*. Jaques does not affect the action in any way, yet his presence darkens the entire mood of Arden. And Touchstone is only a clown, but he is vital to the play's intent. Shakespeare altered his source so that his play is both a pastoral romance and a criticism of pastoral romance. Leslie Hotson (*Shakespeare's Motley*) reveals that the part of Touchstone was not played in the multi-colored suit we associate with clowns but in a long coat of tweed cloth. This looked like the coat worn by a gentleman, which is the reason Corin, Jaques, and William mistake him for one. In Shakespeare's company the part of Touchstone was played by Armin, who had been a goldsmith and, as such, often used touchstones. There is also evidence that the Elizabethans were very familiar with this goldsmith's instrument.

Touchstone is the pivot about whom the play revolves, comments Palmer. The fool puts all things and every person, including himself, to the test. From the beginning we know that he is no respecter of persons and that he has a sense of the fitness of things, as when he tells Le Beau that wrestling is no sport for ladies to watch.

There is no malice in Touchstone. He is genial and genuinely interested in people. For instance, in his conversation with Corin, he really wants to learn about the shepherd (there is no evidence for that in the play); he is not merely mocking him. In assessing Touchstone's place in the play, it is important to note what Shakespeare has him do and what he forbids him to do. For instance, he is never permitted to intrude on the courtship of Orlando and Rosalind, even though he parodies Orlando's verses.

Oscar J. Campbell (*Shakespeare's **Satire***) says that Touchstone is the sound critic of the play, not Jaques. Jaques constantly patronizes Touchstone, completely unaware that Touchstone continually makes fun of him. Touchstone's wooing of Audrey and his eventual marriage is a caricature of the highly inappropriate matches which, as in all romantic comedies, take place at the end of the play.

Barber's view is that Shakespeare is not satirizing actual Elizabethan conditions; he is poking fun at an Elizabethan ideal. But the humor of the play is not really critical of the ideals on which the serious action is founded. Touchstone's comments make fun of an ideal of marriage, not as a bad idea, but one which life does not live up to. (He does not make fun of marriage as such, but of an overly sentimental view of marriage.) The result of having Touchstone represent non-romantic love is not to undercut the play's romance. His exaggerated **realism** forestalls the possible cynicism of the audience towards a play in which one side of love, sex has been ignored. Touchstone may be a critic, but he is also ridiculous when he values his physical comfort more than humility or is attracted to women by his physical needs rather than by their beauty. (The assumption behind this statement is that Shakespeare agrees with the values expressed by Duke Senior, who accepts the pastoral ideal that humility is better than comfort and position - only so long as he is deprived of them, of course.) Touchstone represents one extreme of love, just as Silvius represents another extreme, and these two attitudes are balanced in Rosalind, who combines romantic love with common sense.

Campbell maintains that a study of the play shows that Shakespeare was thoroughly familiar with the contemporary literary fashion of satire. Satirists were assuming the roles of indignant reformers dedicated to exposing vice and corruption, which they claimed to see all about them. Like Jaques, they declared that their criticisms were general and not directed against individuals, and that therefore only those who were guilty would take offense at any particular charge. The intent of such a declaration was, of course, to silence all opposition. Jaques represents Shakespeare's **satire** of these satirists. He is not Shakespeare's mouthpiece in the "Seven Ages" speech, in which his melancholy is a pose and his disgust with the world affected. Although he is usually held up to ridicule, he is occasionally used to make valid satiric comments on the rest of the action.

Parrott sees Jaques in the tradition of the "humor" characters popularized by Ben Jonson. (A humor character is one who continually acts in accordance with a dominant personality trait - in the case of Jaques; his melancholy.) But he adds that Shakespeare, by making Jaques a traveler and a satirist, has taken pains to give him an individual personality. Charlton believes that those who fare worst in Shakespeare's mature comedies are people such as Jaques, who lack genial fellowship with mankind. Jaques does not love anyone; he patronizes everyone. Though he thinks he knows himself and the world, he knows neither. For instance, his "Seven Ages" speech is completely inaccurate, as shown by the events which immediately follow it: the Duke shows charity and Orlando gratitude - two qualities Jaques found no room for in his list. Actually, Jaques is less aware of things than the simple-minded Corin, who is a more profound philosopher than Jaques. (They are really about equally shallow.) Palmer is of the opinion that Jaques is one of those tested by Touchstone. While he thinks he has been amusing himself with a fool, the fool has been amusing himself with Jaques.

Hotson reminds us that, to the Elizabethan ear, Jaques sounded like "jakes" (privy), from which we may gather Shakespeare's attitude toward his character. Jaques is vain, shallow, and a sham. He grows maudlin over the killing of a deer, but he has no scruples about eating it. Along with Frederick and Oliver, Jaques is miraculously transformed at the end of the play, when he blesses the others and admits that there is still something left for him to learn. (His character has certainly mellowed, but not completely changed. Most of his remarks to the wedding couples retain some bite.)

Sen Gupta somewhat modifies the general conception of Jaques. While Jaques plays no part in the action, he is not irrelevant to it. He often corrects the picture of life given by Rosalind, which is something less than the whole picture, which lies between his version and Rosalind's. Jaques' melancholy is not an affectation. If it were, he would sometimes find his pose uncomfortable and in unguarded moments slip out of it into cheerfulness. (But Rosalind, Orlando, and Touchstone all think Jaques is posing, and no one in the play corrects their impression.)

According to Charlton, Rosalind is Shakespeare's ideal lover in the play. Deeply as she falls in love, no person in the play is more aware of the absurdities into which love may lead lovers. Rosalind is constantly aware of her own predicament. She has the gift of inspiring and returning affection, and she is liked by all who know her. She is never artificial and reacts naturally to falling in love. She is fully conscious of what she wants and she is adept in attaining it. Yet with all her accomplishments, she is surprisingly modest. The qualities Parrot finds most outstanding in Rosalind are her naturalness and her simplicity. She only pretends not to know that it was Orlando who carved her name on the trees in Arden, he thinks. (However, Rosalind had no means of knowing that Orlando was in Arden.)

Rosalind stands in no need of correction, except by her own good sense, Palmer thinks. (This is true most of the time, but not always. Touchstone has to correct her sentimentality after she has listened to Silvius' plaint for Phebe. The fool's **parody** about Jane Smile is directed partly at her.) He goes on to say that she is never affected. (Again, this holds true most of the time, but not always. Rosalind, for instance, joins in the "love litany" with the others near the end of the play, and only after a few lines catches herself to call the **refrain** the howling of Irish wolves.) Rosalind, says Stevenson, "has an affection for the absurdities of romantic wooers and encourages these absurdities in Orlando." (Quite the contrary, Rosalind cures Orlando of his absurdities.)

In Sen Gupta's view, there is not much subtlety in the portrayal of individual characters. For instance, there is really no obstacle to Rosalind's marrying Orlando at once, when she meets him in Arden and finds out he loves her. (But there are at least two obstacles:

1. Rosalind must find out whether Orlando really does love her, or whether he is just talking about love.

2. Rosalind must cure Orlando of his sentimental notions about love.

But she delights in playing a cat and mouse game with her lover, enabling her to demonstrate her wit, but also demonstrating "the essential emptiness of the central **episode** in the story." Rosalind's capabilities are never put to any real test, so that she seems to be "brilliant but superficial." He concludes that the fault lies in Shakespeare's attempt to express character in too thin a plot.

Evans asserts that, even without disguise, Rosalind's natural gifts would give her an advantage over everyone else in the play. The gap between Rosalind and Orlando, he finds, is the gap between "omniscience" and "oblivion." Not that Orlando is a stupid man, Evans hastens to add, he is just oblivious. (The distinction between never knowing what is going on and being stupid is not too clear.) Orlando is repeatedly exposed to situations where the truth eludes him, before he ever meets Rosalind. Ludicrous comments are continually being made about him, such as Celia's telling Rosalind that she found Orlando under a tree, like a dropped acorn. Evans continues that Orlando's "abrupt disposal of Charles" at his first meeting with Rosalind, after which he cannot put in a single word for himself, his "frightfully unaware" entrance to demand food of the Duke, and the samples of his verse, all prepare us to think of Orlando as no more than a "sturdy booby." (What Orlando's overthrow of Charles has to do with his intelligence is difficult to see, as is the difference between his being stupid and a "sturdy booby.")

Palmer says that one person who does not need Touchstone's correction is the Duke. He is never deceived by pastoral life; he corrects himself. (The Duke is very obviously deceived in his expectations of pastoral life which he praises in the conventional fashion. But even when he realizes the truth about pastoralism, he keeps up the pretense that it is what it is not. He does not correct himself, but rather gives away his true feelings on a number of occasions. He is corrected by Touchstone, whose sour comment on Arden is a reply to the Duke's praise.)

AS YOU LIKE IT

ESSAY QUESTIONS AND ANSWERS

Question: What does Shakespeare satirize in the play and what are the techniques of **satire** he uses?

Answer: Shakespeare satirizes pastoral love, the entire pastoral ideal, satirists, Englishmen who return from abroad to criticize their own country, and the elaborate code of quarreling of the time.

Shakespeare's **satire** of pastoral love is carried out through the exaggerated behavior of Orlando, Oliver and Celia, Silvius and Phebe; through the commentary of Touchstone, as well as by Touchstone's **parody** in marrying Audrey; and by the commentary of Rosalind. As soon as Orlando falls in love with Rosalind, he is struck dumb. Had all lovers in pastoral romance been so affected by the sight of their ladies, much ink would have been saved, for they usually spend an enormous amount of time declaring how much they suffer in love. Orlando goes from one extreme to the other. In Arden he finds his tongue again, so much so that he decorates the trees of the forest with bad love poems to Rosalind. (The poetry is so bad that Touchstone has no trouble in parodying the meter at great length.) Orlando has evidently read too many pastoral romances, for he knows all the conventional attitudes he should assume. He is convinced, for instance, that if Rosalind should only once frown at him, he would probably drop dead.

Another **satire** on pastoral love is the obvious exaggeration of Oliver's whirlwind romance with Celia and their decision to marry the day after they have met. But the focal point of the play's **satire** is concentrated on Silvius and Phebe, the stock pastoral characters. He can think of nothing but his love, and he certainly cannot be bothered with looking after sheep. He is constantly scorned by his lady, and he is fully convinced that he is not really worthy of her love, even though he is a very handsome man and she is rather plain. Although his lady says she does not love him, he is so humble in her presence that he will be content if only she will pity him, and he too, like Orlando, thinks that one frown from his lady would kill him. Phebe is the stock heroine of romance. Even though she really likes Silvius - she has no hesitation in marrying him in the end - she coldly rejects all his advances because that is what the **convention** said she should do. But then she herself falls so hopelessly in love that she forgets all about the **conventions** and not only allows another man to woo her but does not wait for him to begin; she runs after him and openly declares how much in love she is. Then the great love of her life turns out to be misplaced: Ganymede is revealed as Rosalind.

Much of the play's **satire** is provided by Touchstone. The tool is exaggeration. When Silvius sighs his heart out for Phebe so feelingly that even the level-headed Rosalind is touched, Touchstone sweeps away the aura of sentimentality by recalling a wildly improbable love affair he had with a milkmaid. When

Rosalind is impressed by the sentimental slush Orlando has written in her praise, Touchstone demonstrates the superficial quality of such "poetry" by composing a **parody** of it on the spot. His most outstanding parody of pastoral love is marriage to Audrey. While the others married for romance, he marries for sex. Rosalind satirizes the conventional view of love by her comments to Phebe and her lessons for Orlando. She urges Phebe to get down on her knees and thank heaven for sending her such a man as Silvius; the pastoral **convention** taught that the lover should kneel to his lady and beg her for pity. When Orlando swears that he is about to die for love of Rosalind, she coolly tells him, "Men have died from time to time and worms have eaten them, but not for love." The pastoral ideal taught that the court and city were corrupt, but that the country was pure and a place where good men would find contentment. The country figures of Elizabethan fiction are always extremely polished and eloquent. This view of pastoral life is satirized through the comments of Duke Senior, Jaques, and Touchstone, and through the persons of Corin, William, and Audrey. The Duke tries desperately to make himself believe that it is really much better to wander about Arden than to be a Duke in his own palace. He talks at length about the fact that in the forest no one will flatter him and no one, certainly, will plot against him as his brother had done. But he himself reveals to us that he is talking more to keep his courage up than out of conviction. After he hears of the plight of Orlando and Adam, he lets slip the remark that other people are evidently just as unhappy as he is. When news comes of his brother's conversation, he hastens back to Court, sacrificing his pastoral paradise.

Touchstone, through his conversations with Corin, William, and Audrey, demonstrates that real country people are not at all the polished and eloquent lovers represented in pastoral romance.

Shakespeare's **satire** of satirists is manifested in the actions and statements of Jaques. He comes off quite badly in his contact with all the other characters, who find his continual criticism neither amusing nor clever. Even the not-very-bright Orlando can outwit him.

Question: What is typically Elizabethan about *As You Like It*?

Answer: The objects of the **satire**, the licensed fool, women disguised as men, dialogue which indicates scenery, soliloquies and asides, the love poems, the **blank verse** in which most of the play is written, the puns and sexual **allusions** of the dialogue, and the songs are typically Elizabethan. What the play makes fun of - the love of reading pastoral romances, the pastoral ideal, satirists, malcontent travelers, the code of quarreling - all are typically Elizabethan. The idea of having a court jester as commentator on the action of the play originated with Shakespeare. The disguising of women as men derives from the Elizabethan custom of having female parts played by boy actors; the audience was amused by the thought of a boy playing a woman's part who was pretending to be a man - they loved complication. Because the Elizabethan stage had no scenery, the scenery had to be indicated in the dialogue of the characters, such as Rosalind's, "Well, this is the forest of Arden." The **convention** of the soliloquy, in which a character tells the audience what he is thinking, is also typically Elizabethan. Orlando's love poems speak of Rosalind as the typical sonneteer of the period spoke of his lady: Rosalind is the sum of all female virtues which have existed since the beginning of time. **Blank verse** (unrimed iambic **pentameter**) is the hallmark of Elizabethan drama, having been popularized by Christopher Marlowe at the beginning of Shakespeare's career. The elaborate use of puns is another trademark of Elizabethan drama. The Elizabethans liked puns because they were proud of their language and its various shades of meaning. The boldness - and sometimes coarseness - of the jokes on sex reflects the temper of the time; people who were not squeamish about public executions liked their humor robust. Finally, the songs of the play testify to the Elizabethan love of music. It was an age when almost everyone sang or played some musical instrument.

Question: What are the important love or friendship relationships in the play, and what are their functions?

Answer: The play has two primary friendships and four groups of lovers. In terms of plot, the friendship between Celia and Rosalind gives the latter a confidante in Arden. From the point of view of satiric intent, Rosalind and Celia are the inseparable friends of the conventional romance, except for the fact that such a friendship was always between men. The other friendship is the one between Orlando and Adam, which makes us think well of Orlando from the beginning. In Adam's exaggerated devotion to Orlando there is also some satiric intent: Adam is the loyal follower who the Elizabethans liked to think existed in the "good old days" when servants were content to serve their masters for pure love.

The play's main love relationship is between Orlando and Rosalind. In terms of entertainment - something Shakespeare always had an eye for - it provides the play with some honest-to-goodness romance and a lot of humor. In terms of **satire**, it is an education for Orlando, as he gets rid of some of his sentimental notions about love. The Silvius-Phebe relationship exists purely for satiric purposes: it is a demonstration of how ridiculous pastoral love can be. The Oliver-Celia match is one of convenience. Celia cannot be left single at the end - an unthinkable situation in a romantic comedy. It also serves to make fun of similar whirlwind romances in Elizabethan fiction.

The Touchstone-Audrey farce is, of course, a satiric contrast to the extreme romanticism of Silvius and Phebe and, to a lesser extent, of the others.

Question: What is the function of Touchstone in the play?

Answer: Touchstone's function is to reveal the true nature of the other characters in the play and to expose sham wherever he finds it. He illuminates the natures of Rosalind, Orlando, Celia, Jaques, Duke Senior, Corin, William, and Audrey. He exposes the artificiality of pastoral love and conventional quarreling. The fact that Touchstone has so much affection for Celia tells us something about her character as Adam's affection tells us about Orlando. Touchstone's fondness for Celia is a sign that Celia is not affected and does not take herself too seriously.

When Jaques and Touchstone first meet in the forest, Jaques is deceived by Touchstone's outward appearance and assumes because Touchstone wears the costume of a fool he must therefore be foolish. Jaques' stupidity is revealed when Touchstone starts spouting philosophy. What Touchstone is really doing is mimicking Jaques, and what he says is just as shallow as what Jaques says. But Jaques is extremely impressed with Touchstone's nonsense.

Duke Senior, on the other hand, realizes Touchstone's true wit, and thus shows himself to be much more perceptive than Jaques.

The conversations of Touchstone with Corin, William, and Audrey put an end to the myth - perpetuated in pastoral romance - that shepherds were elegant and learned people who possessed some secret wisdom denied to those who lived in the city.

Question: What is the function of Rosalind's disguise in the play?

Answer: Rosalind's disguise serves a number of functions. First, it amuses the spectators because they know that the actor is a boy. The added complication of having him play a girl pretending to be a boy provides added enjoyment and confusion. Second, the disguise also provides the play with dramatic irony: the audience has information that some of the actors do not have, namely, the fact that Ganymede is really Rosalind. Thus the audience is able to share Rosalind's enjoyment when Orlando woos her in place of Rosalind, and all the time is talking to Rosalind herself. A second bit of dramatic **irony** the audience enjoys as a result of Rosalind's disguise is Phebe's falling in love with Rosalind disguised as Ganymede. Here is Phebe who has so long scorned love, and when she finally falls head over heels in love it is with a woman disguised as a man! Third, her disguise allows Rosalind to reverse the conventional roles of man and woman; instead of Orlando's pursuing her, she can pursue him by constantly reminding him of his love for Rosalind. It should be noted that, in so doing, she accomplishes the opposite of what she has promised Orlando she will do, for she had said that she would cure him of his love for Rosalind. Fourth, it allows Rosalind to rid Orlando of his too sentimental notions about love, and lastly, her disguise permits her to find out whether Orlando really is in love, or whether he just says he is.

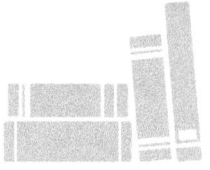

BIBLIOGRAPHY

TOUCHSTONE

Goldsmith, R. H., "Touchstone: Critic in Motley," *PMLA*, LXVIII (Sept., 1953), 884-895.

Hillis, Robert, *Wise Fools in Shakespeare*, 1955.

Hodgson, Geraldine, "Shakespeare's Fools," *Church Quarterly Review*, CXIII (1932), 209-223.

Hotson, Leslie, *Shakespeare's Motley*, 1952.

Sitwell, E., "Of the Clowns and Fools of Shakespeare," *Life and Letters*, LVII (May, 1948), 102-109.

Welsford, Enid, *The Fool*, 1961.

JAQUES

Bennett, Josephine W., "Jaques' Seven Ages," *Shakespeare Association Bulletin*, XVIII (Oct., 1943), 168-174.

Jones, J. T., "What's That Ducdame?" *Modern Language Notes*, LXII (Dec., 1947), 563-4.

Peattie, Elia (Wilkinson), *How Jaques Came into the Forest of Arden,* 1901.

Wilcox, John, "Putting Jaques into *As You Like It*," *Modern Language Review*, XXXVI (July, 1941), 388-394.

MISCELLANEOUS CHARACTERS

Brooks, Charles, "Shakespeare's Heroine Actresses," *Shakespeare Jahrbuch*, 1960.

Draper, J. W., "Shakespeare's Orlando Innamorato," *Modern Language Quarterly*, II (June, 1941) 179-184.

McCloskey, John C., "Fear of the People as a Minor Motive in Shakespeare," *Shakespeare Association Bulletin*, XVII (April, 1942), 68-72.

Sampley, Arthur M., "A Warning-Piece Against Shakespeare's Women," *Shakespeare Association Bulletin*, XV (Jan. 1940), 34-39.

Watson, Curtis B., "Shakespeare's Dukes," *Shakespeare Association Bulletin*, XVI (Jan., 1941), 33-41.

SOME AVAILABLE PAPERBACKS

Byrne, M. St. Clare, *Elizabethan Life in Town and Country,* University.

Chute, Marchette, *Shakespeare of London*, Everyman.

Clemen, Wolfgang, T*he Development of Shakespeare's* **Imagery**, Drama-books.

Dean, L. F., *Shakespeare: Modern Essays in Criticism,* Oxford.

Harbage, Alfred, *William Shakespeare: a Reader's Guide,* Noonday

Joseph, Sister Miriam, *Rhetoric in Shakespeare's Time,* Harbinger.

Mason, Dorothy E., *Music in Elizabethan England,* Cornell.

Spencer, Theodore, *Shakespeare and the Nature of Man,* Macmillan.

Stoll, E. E., *Art and Artifice in Shakespeare,* Barnes & Noble.

Tillyard, E. M. W., *The Elizabethan World Picture,* Vintage.

SUBJECTS FOR RESEARCH AND ANALYSIS

A comparison between *As You Like It* and its source, Lodge's *Rosalynde.*

A comparison of As You Like It with Twelfth Night and Much Ado About Nothing.

A comparison between Shakespeare's romantic comedies and "problem" comedies.

A comparison between the function of the fool in Shakespearian comedy and tragedy.

A comparison between the function of disguise of identity in Shakespearean comedy and disguise of personality in tragedy.

The influence of Shakespeare's stage on the writing of *As You Like It.*

The influence of the actors in Shakespeare's company on the writing of *As You Like It.*

Elizabethan satire.

Elizabethan pastoral romance.

The Elizabethan courtier.

The function of song in Shakespeare's plays.

The sources of Jaques' "Seven Ages" speech.

www.ingramcontent.com/pod-product-compliance
Lightning Source LLC
LaVergne TN
LVHW011716060526
838200LV00051B/2916